THE FIGURE DRAWINGS OF
JEFFREY R. WATTS

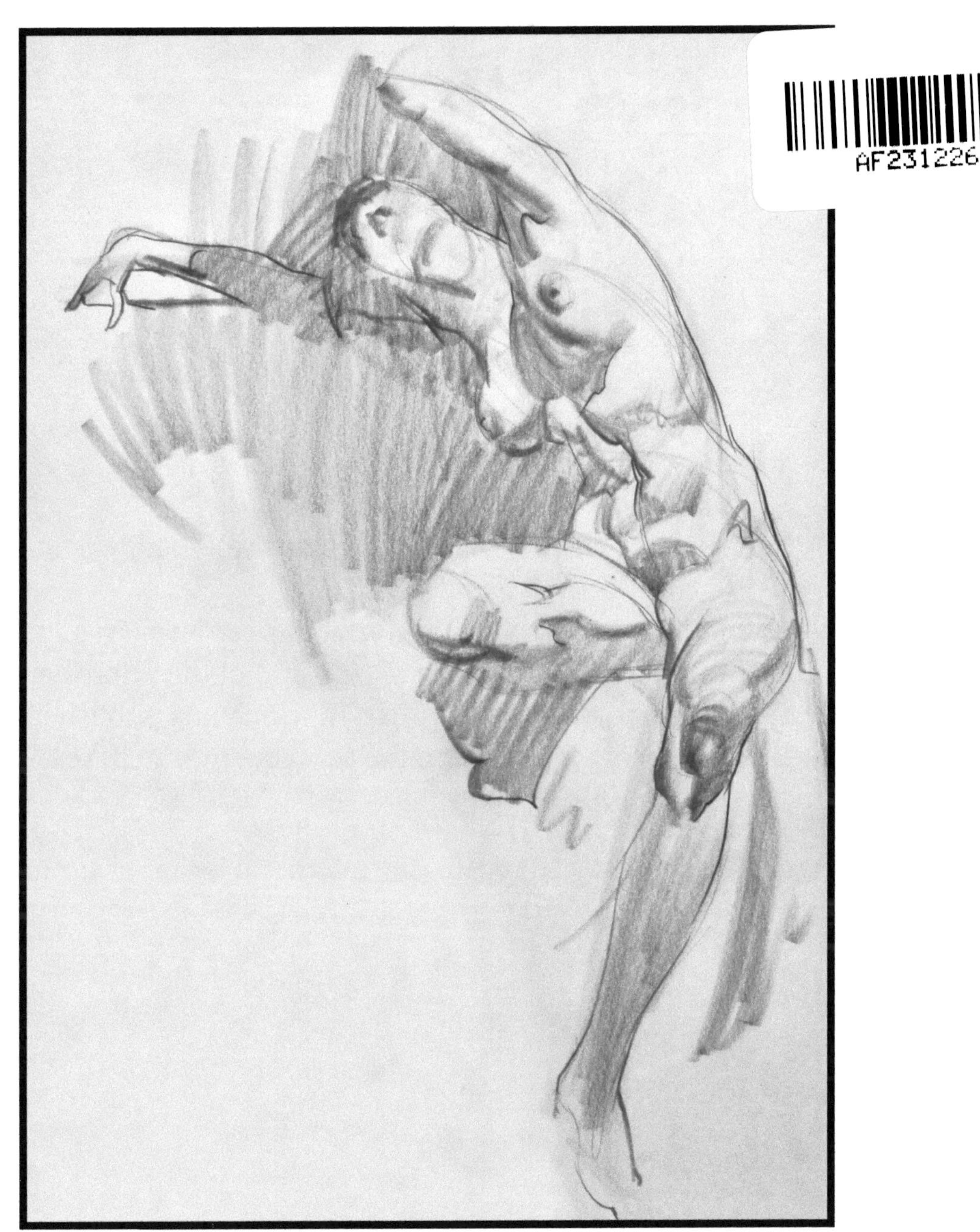

VOLUME 2
FEMALE QUICKSKETCH

THE FIGURE DRAWINGS OF
JEFFREY R. WATTS

VOLUME 2
FEMALE QUICKSKETCH

ISBN: 978-0-9903735-3-7

Published By:
Leucadia Publishing, LLC
171 Calle Magdalena STE 101
Encinitas, Calif., 92024

This edition: September 2021

Printed by Ingram | Lightning Source in one of several locations around the world.

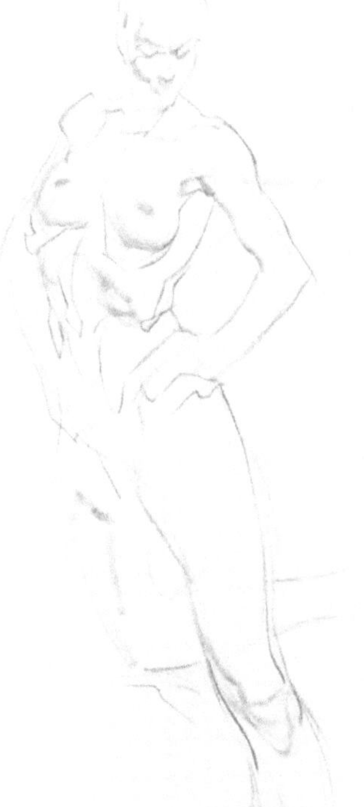

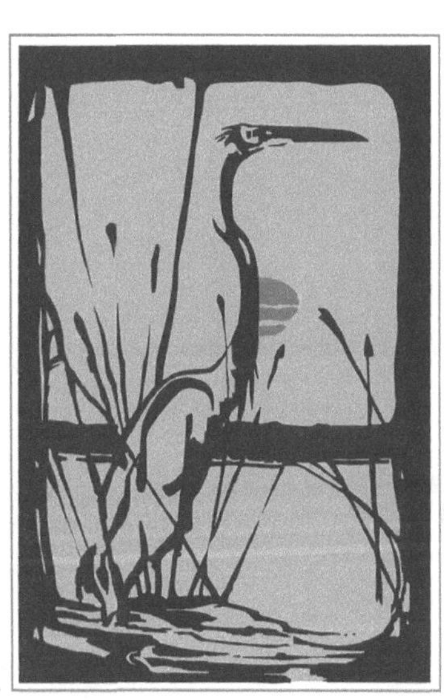

LEUCADIA
PUBLISHING LLC
ART · VISION · EDUCATION

FORWARD

Jeff Watts is an art educator from Southern California. For the past 30 years he has run Watts Atelier of the Arts with his wife Krista. Throughout his 30 year art career he has worked for some of the biggest names in entertainment as well as received numerous awards for his work in many different exhibitions. More than a decade ago, he aspired to develop the Watts Atelier Online Program, bringing the concentrated learning environment from the Atelier to the internet. After years of hard work the online community is continuing to grow, with over 1000 hours of demos and instruction on the fundamentals of art.

This book was created in the hopes that art students would have a resource to go to when looking to study the human figure. It was my experience when I was an art student that there was a great shortage of proficient drawings from which to study and emulate the more subtle aspects of figure drawing such as calligraphy, idealization, accurate value and edges.

Try to use these drawings to bridge the gap from more rigid academic anatomical studies to more artistic anatomy. It has been my experience over the last 30 plus years of drawing from life that the best drawings I have executed contain 3 parts; part what I see; part what I know, and part what I wish I saw. I wish you all the joy that drawing the human form has brought me over the decades, for there is no better designed machine. Trying to do justice to this magnificent engineering marvel was the intention of this book. Happy drawing.

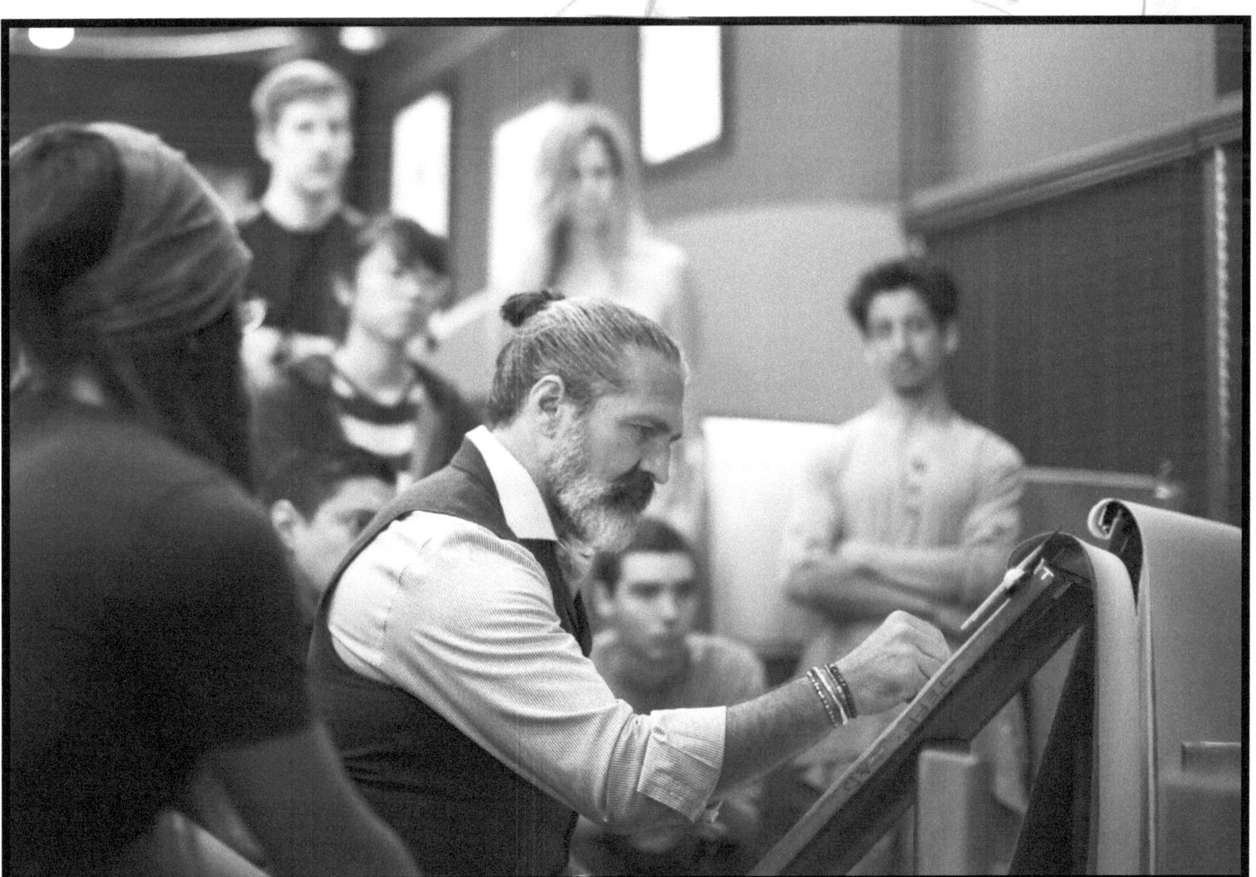

WHAT IS QUICKSKETCH?

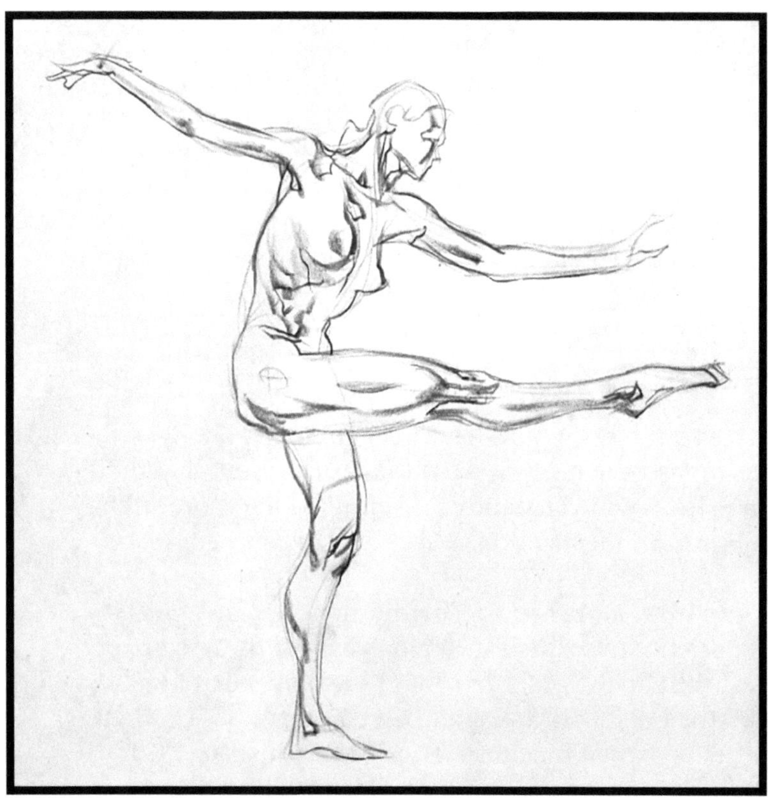

At its core, quicksketch is drawing the figure in a short time frame. Poses are typically only held for 1-5 minutes and the focus is on portraying a quick indication of the model.

The way we do quicksketch is deeply rooted in the Reilly Method; a system of drawing that seeks to efficiently identify the action of the pose through the use of a rhythmical grid system.

If you see an experienced draftsman in the act of quicksketch you will notice that they do not move with speed, but with slow, methodical and calculated efficiency.

I'm a bit of a different story. I have done this so much that I can draw quicksketch quick! It can almost look like a magic trick, but the only reason that I can do this is from tens of thousands of drawings. Most of them done slowly and calculated. If you watch me do this on video (link for a course is available on the last page) I would say don't follow my lead in terms of speed. What you'll want to look for is how I go about building up the drawing.

WHY QUICKSKETCH?

Quicksketch can be used for many different things. It depends on where you are at in your training and what you're trying to learn. At the heart of it, quicksketch is used to build quick analyzation skills; to interpret the figure quickly and accurately. Through the use of the Reilly Method you will develop an intuitive nature for understanding the way that any form can rhythmically tie together. On top of that, you'll learn how to intuitively measure proportions and suggest volumes through quick indications.

An advanced student will be proficient at getting the basic gestures and rhythms down. From there you can move into more advanced study. It would be highly beneficial for a student to use quicksketch to study how an arm works, how the torso wedges, how the legs are constructed or even the complexities of the back. As you delve into deeper study of the figure, use quicksketch to buff out your intuitive anatomy skills with concepts learned from books like

Watts on Bridgman (my own book on studying the works of George B. Bridgman) as well as *Figure Drawing for All its Worth* by Andrew Loomis and *Figure Drawing: Design and Invention* by Michael Hampton, to name a few.

FUNDAMENTALS, NOT FLASH.

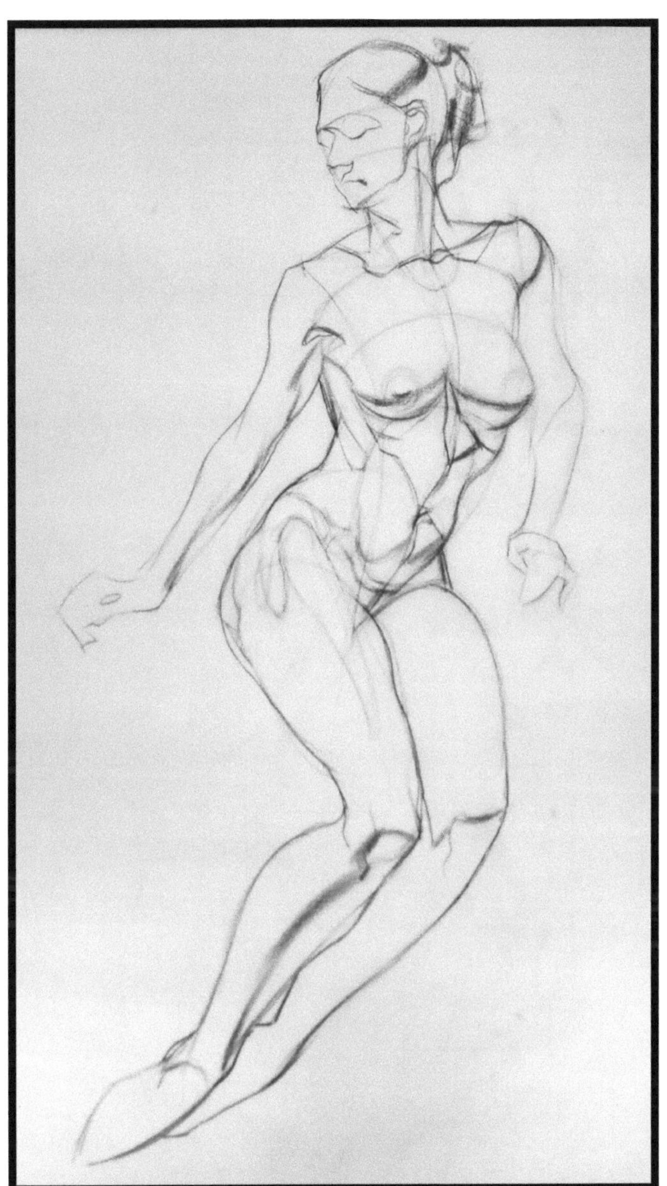 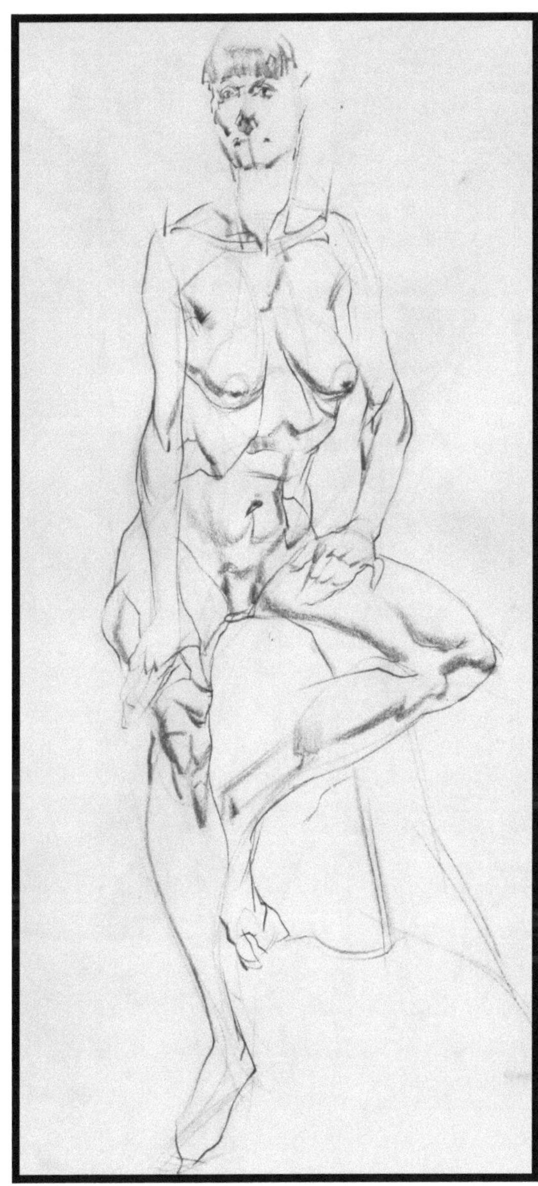

Compare the drawings above. Notice the very simple approach on the left, and the more complex mapping and design on the right. Most of the work in this book is complex, so you'll need to filter it though simplicity. Strive for a simple rhythmical statement in your quicksketches when you start. Once you get more comfortable with the process you can then move into my more advanced calligraphy (the look of my work; my style) and try to break down how and why I make the decisions that I make.

Quicksketch can be very challenging, so be compassionate with yourself as you go through this process. Believe it or not, quicksketch was the hardest thing for me to learn. I spent thousands of hours over decades practicing to become masterful. You can too, it's all about the work.

THE ORIGINAL REILLY ABSTRACTIONS
HANDOUTS BY FRED FIXLER

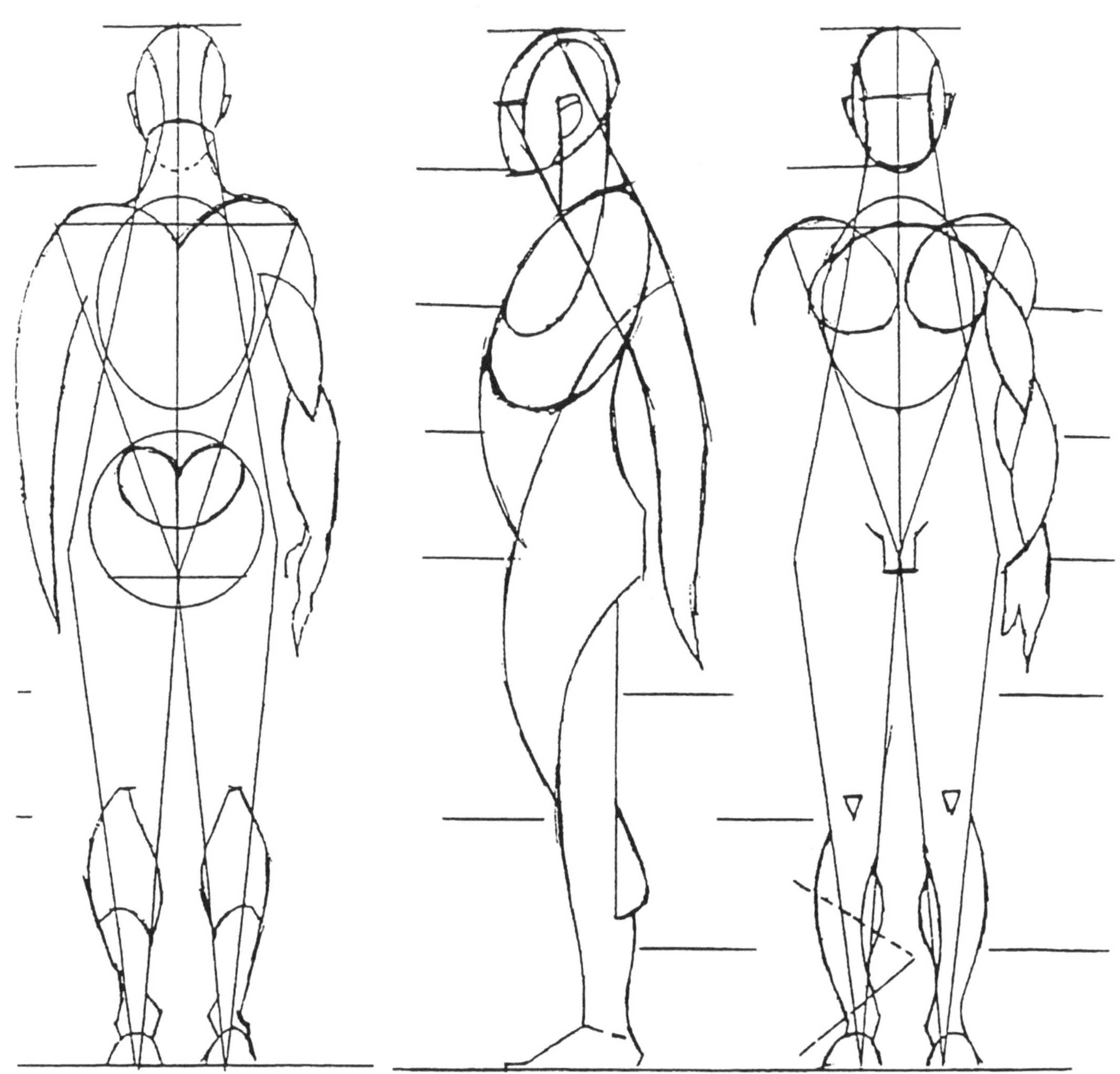

The above Reilly Abstractions were the ones that were given to me when I was first studying at the California Art Institute in Calabasas. As you can see, they are very simple. They provide the basis from which I designed the more complex abstractions on the next page.

I wanted to take the essence of the Reilly Method and marry it with the anatomy of the human form. The tying together and flow from piece to piece should not stop with the biggest forms of the body. Developing this more complex version has allowed me to find smaller sub-rhythms in the body to aid flow, movement and design. Using the version I created will allow anatomical knowledge to be further ingrained and memorized.

ADVANCED REILLY ABSTRACTIONS
REDESIGNED BY JEFF WATTS

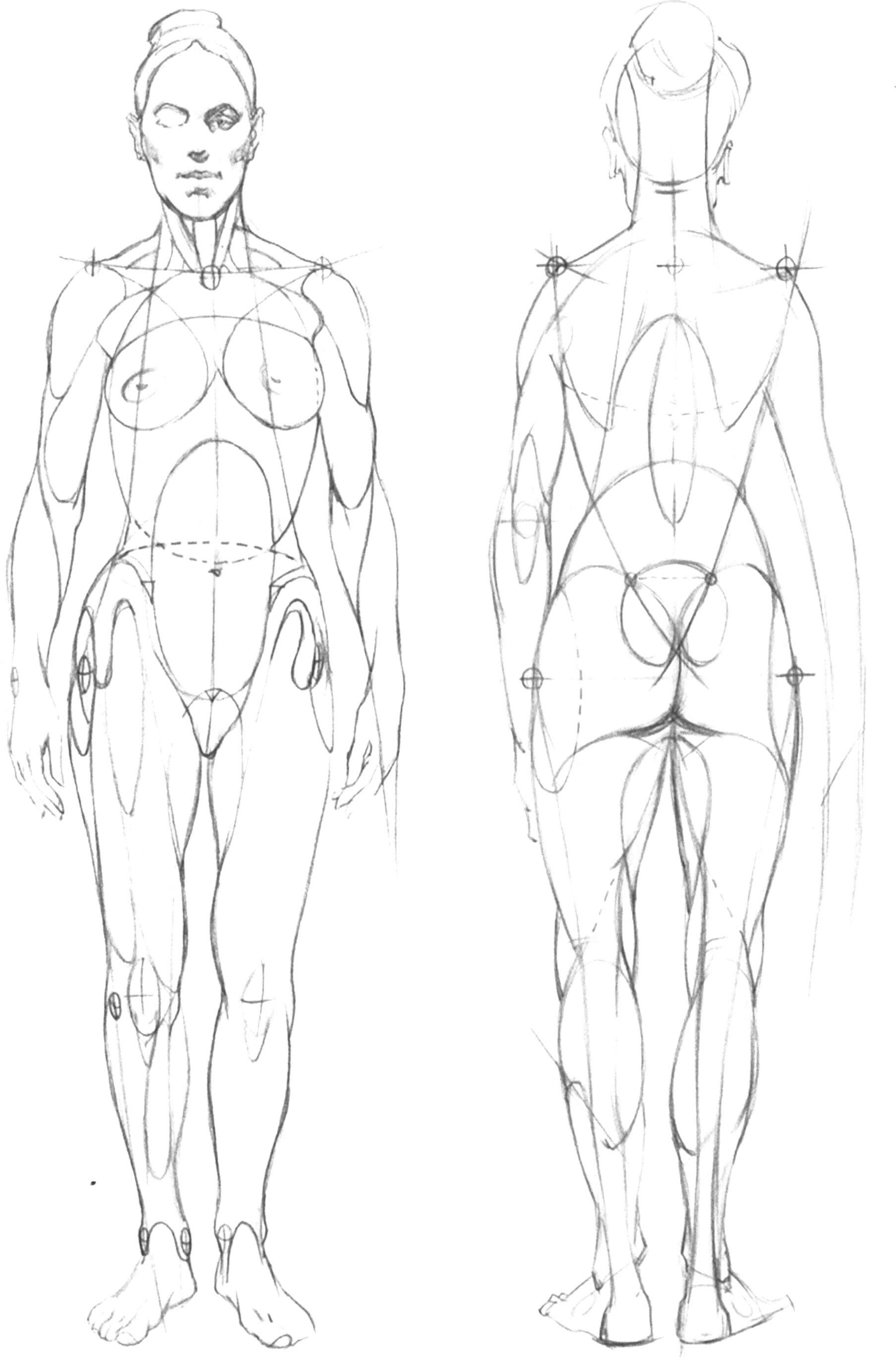

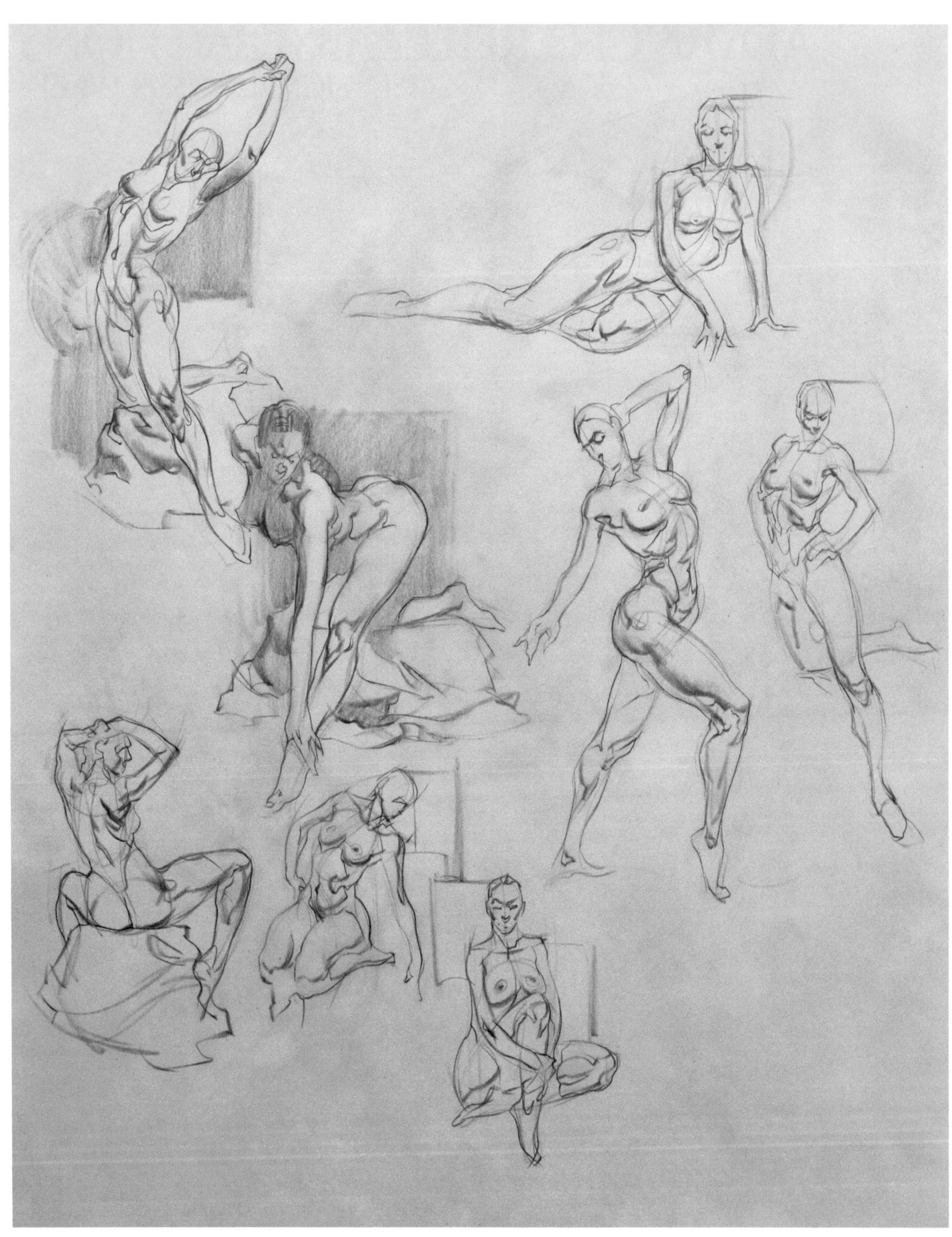

18x24
Charcoal/Newsprint
Quicksketch

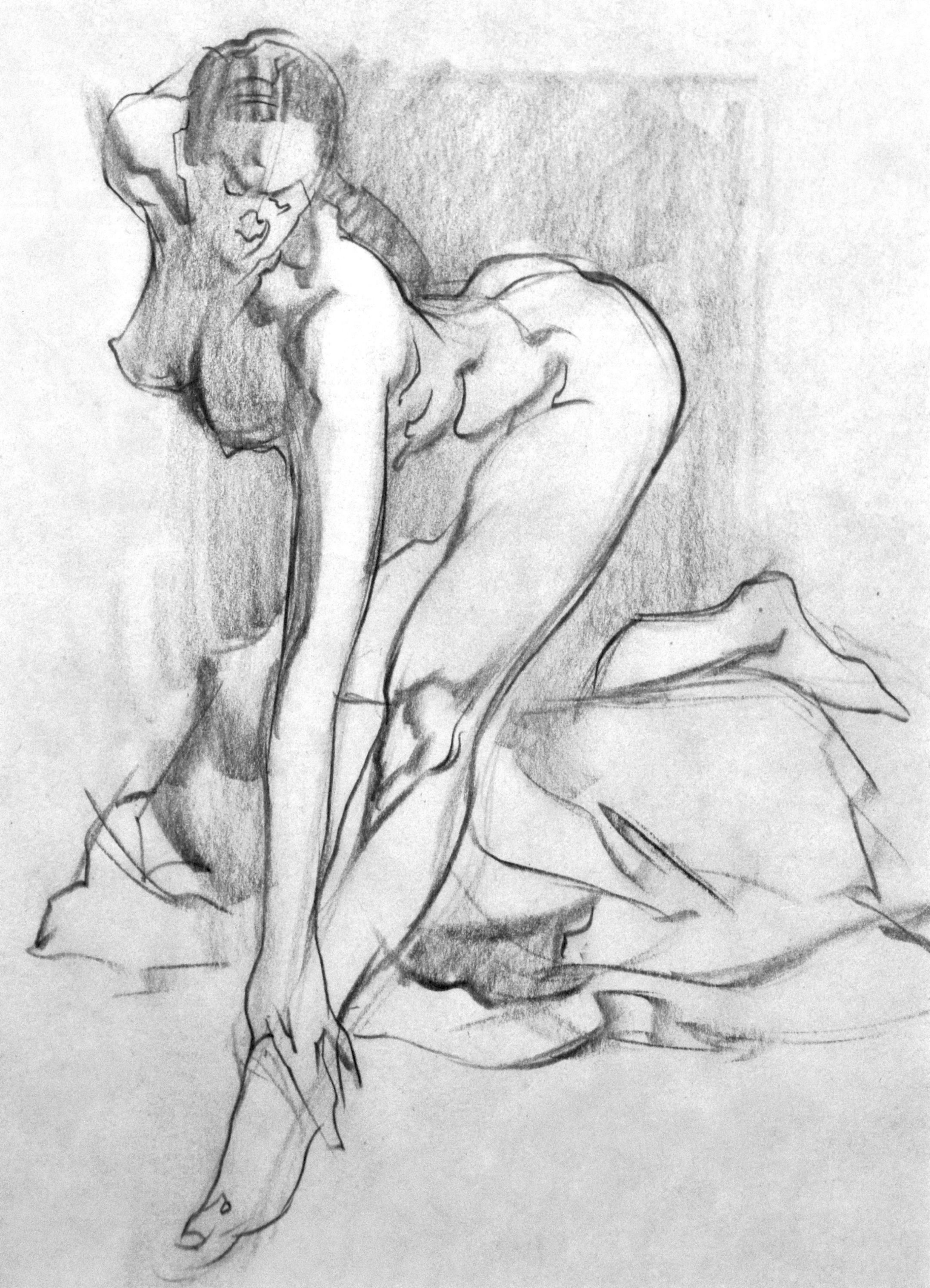

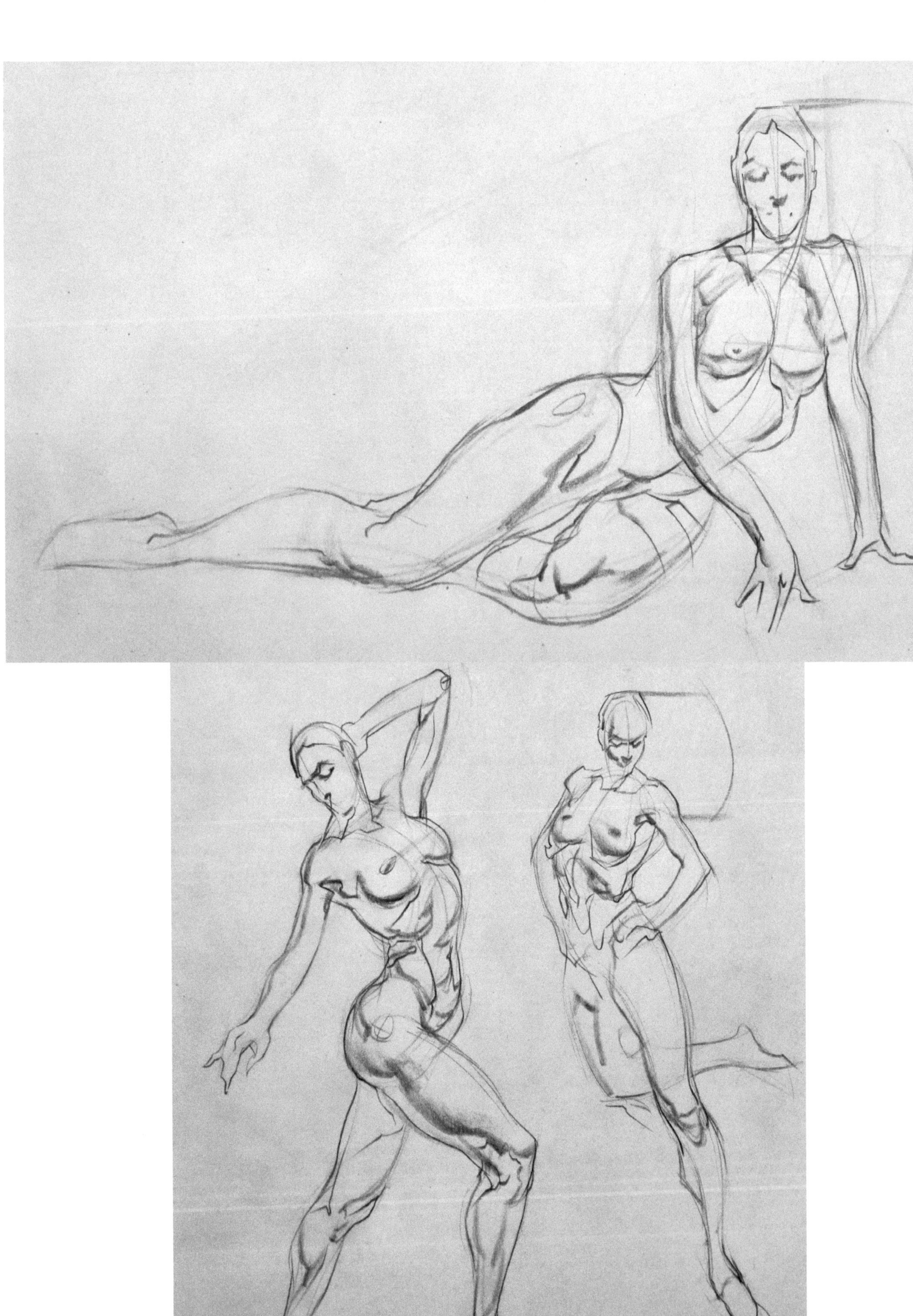

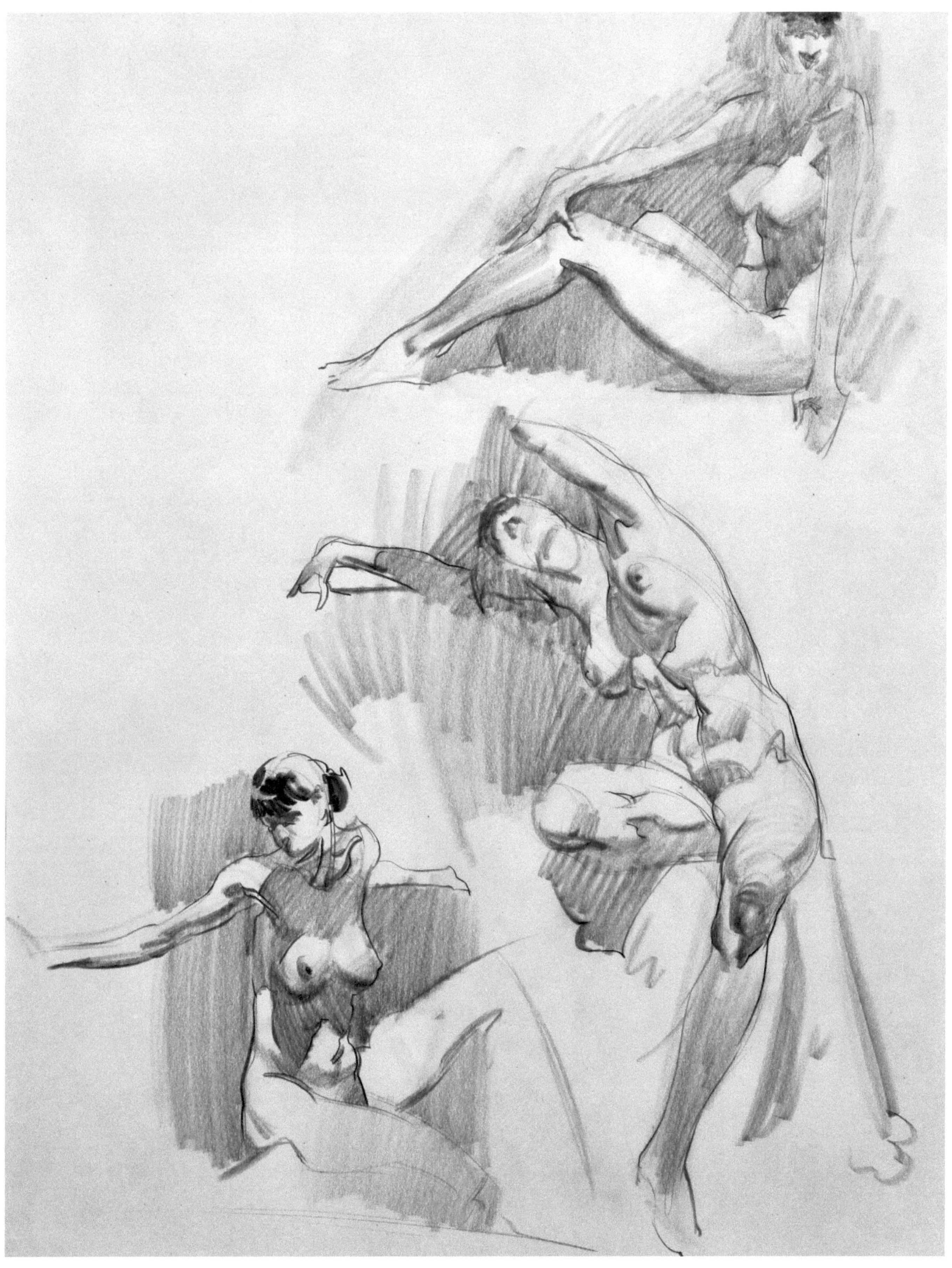

18x24
Charcoal/Newsprint
Quicksketch

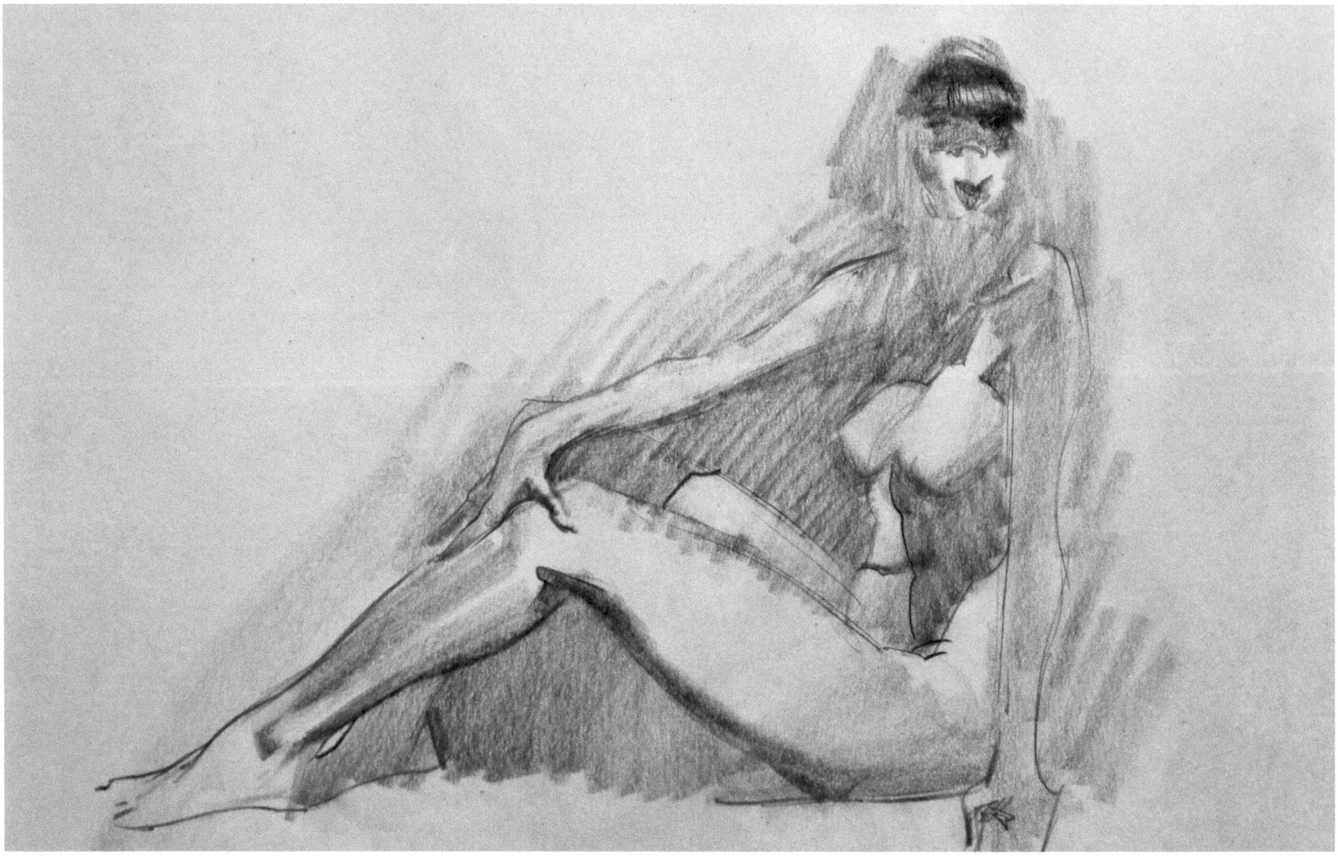

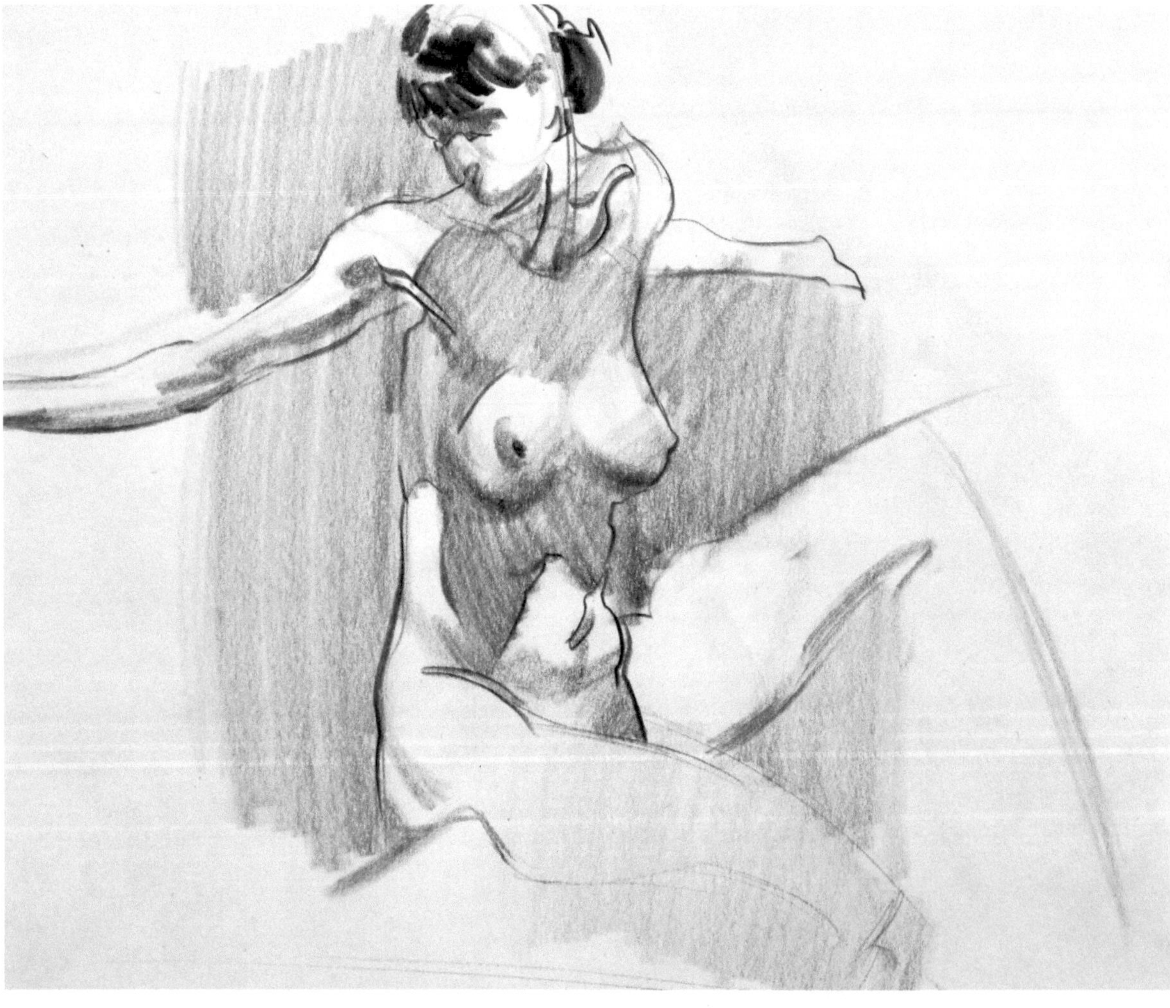

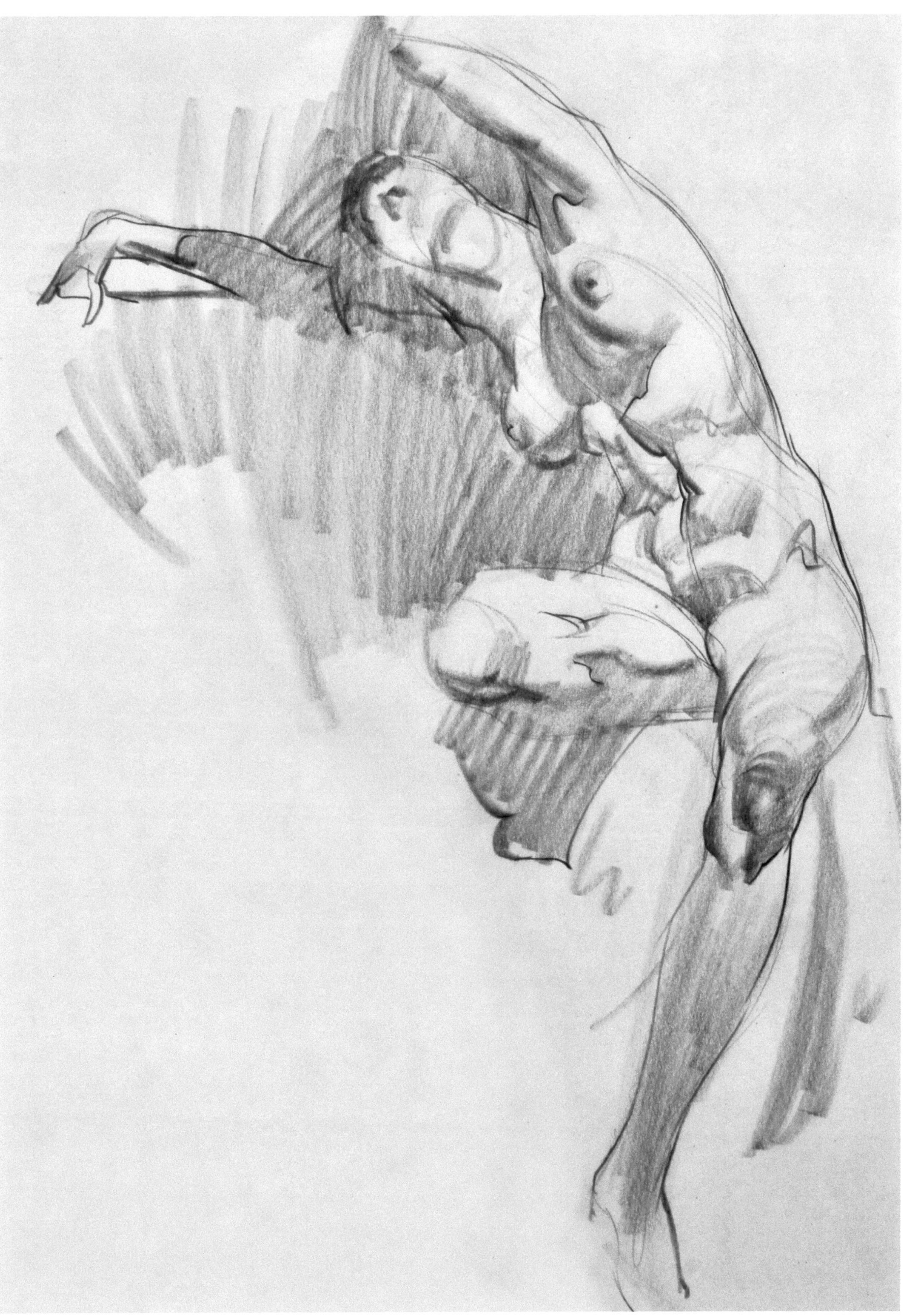

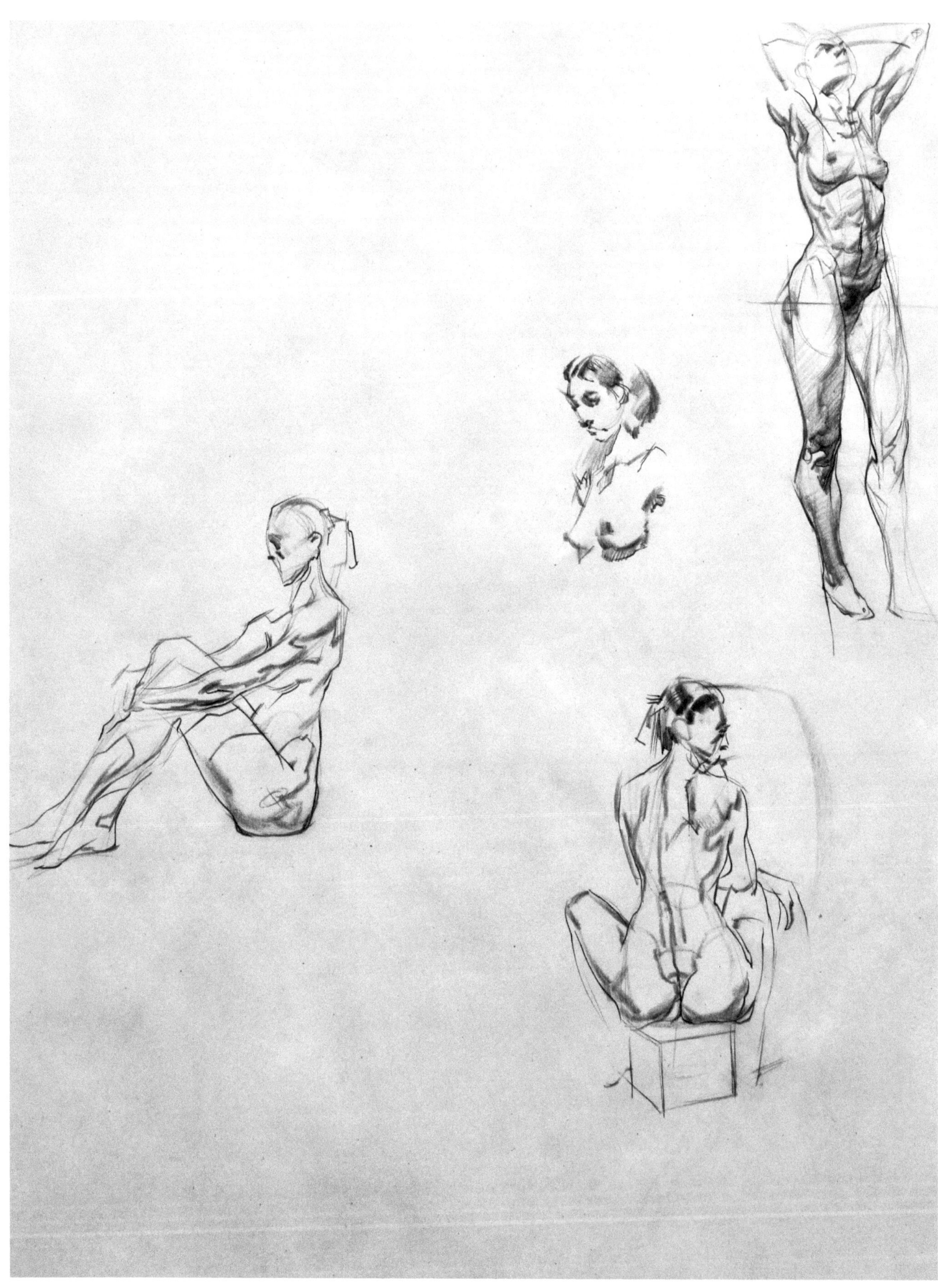

18x24
Charcoal/Newsprint
Quicksketch

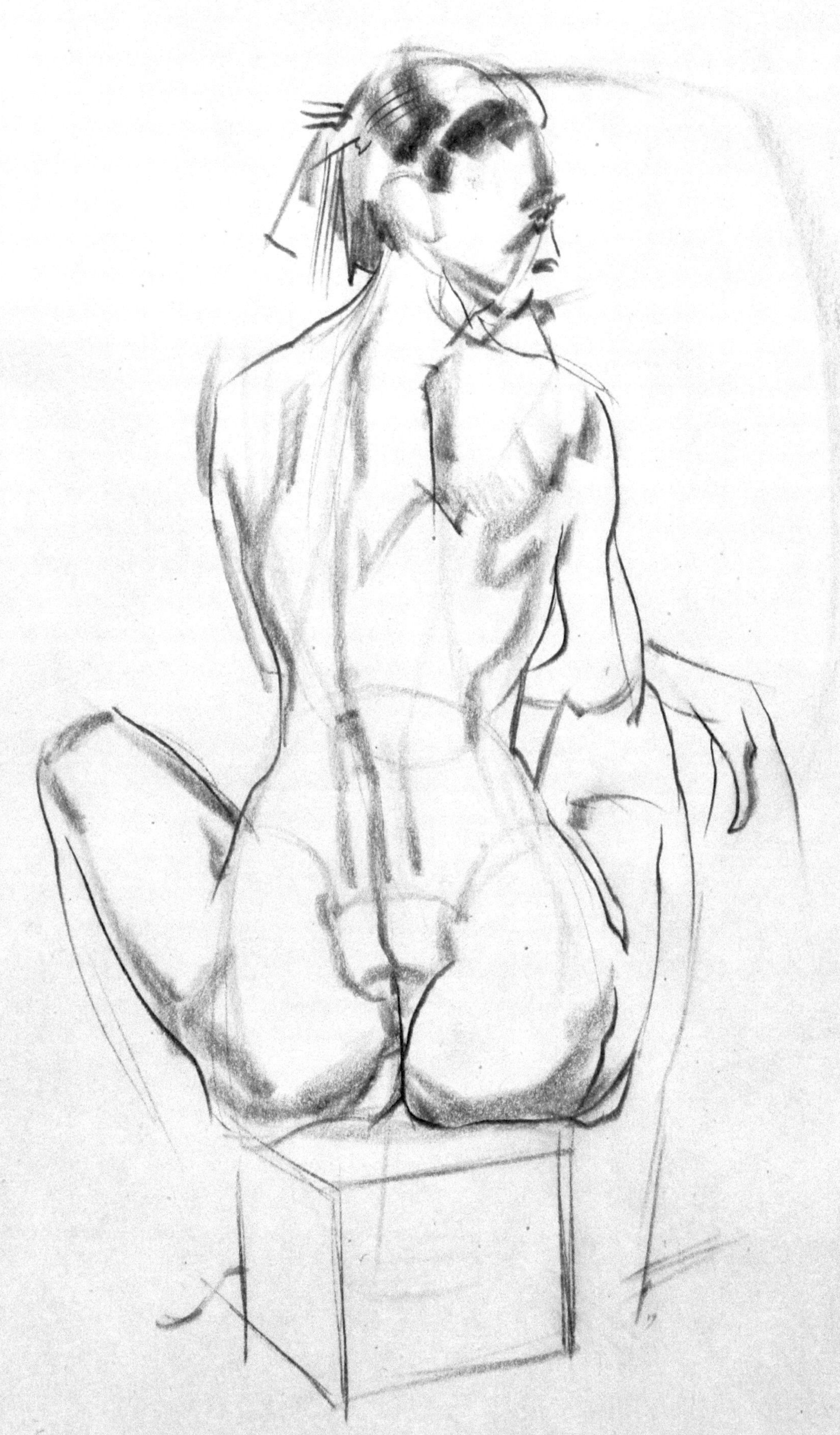

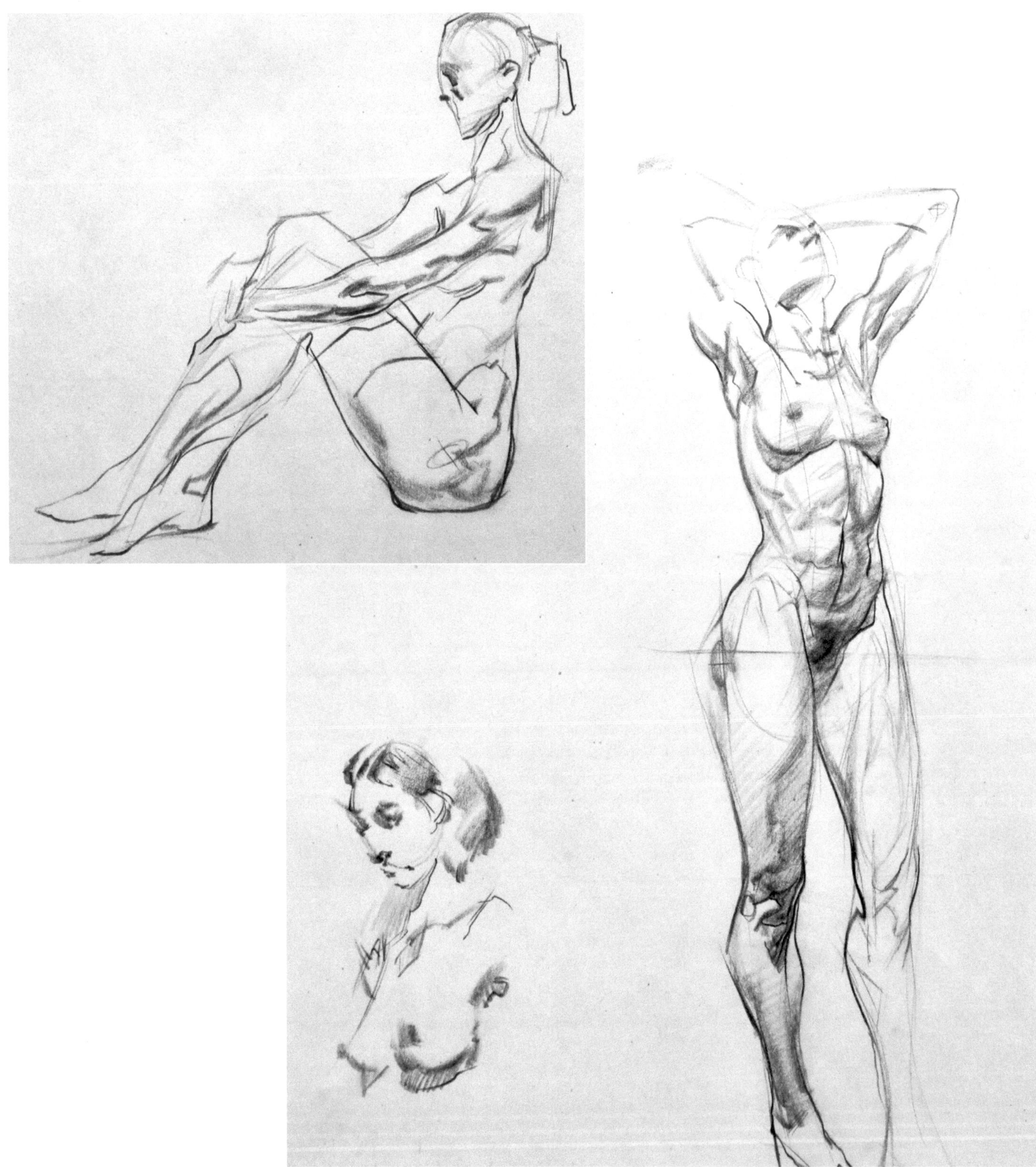

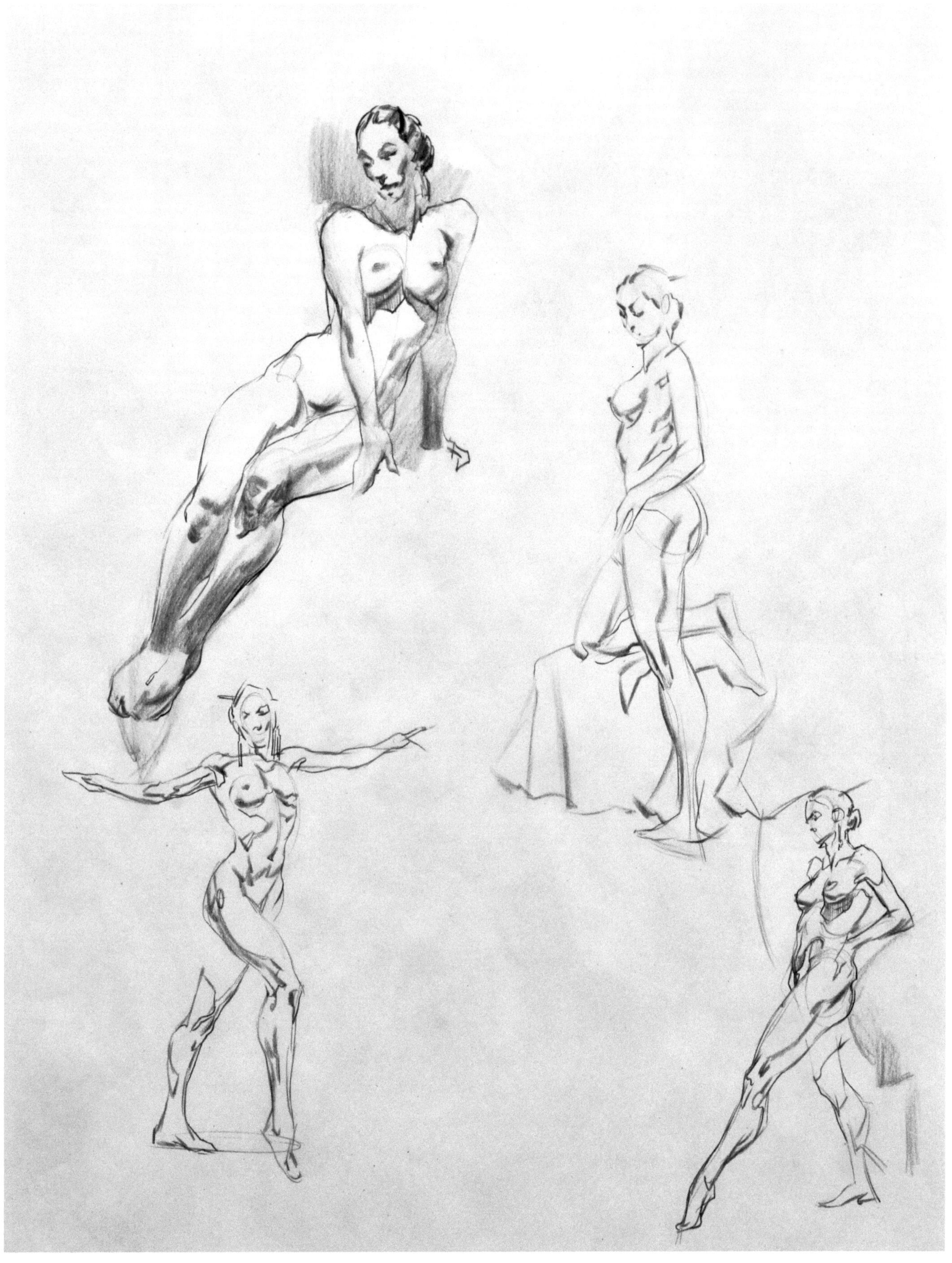

18x24
Charcoal/Newsprint
Quicksketch

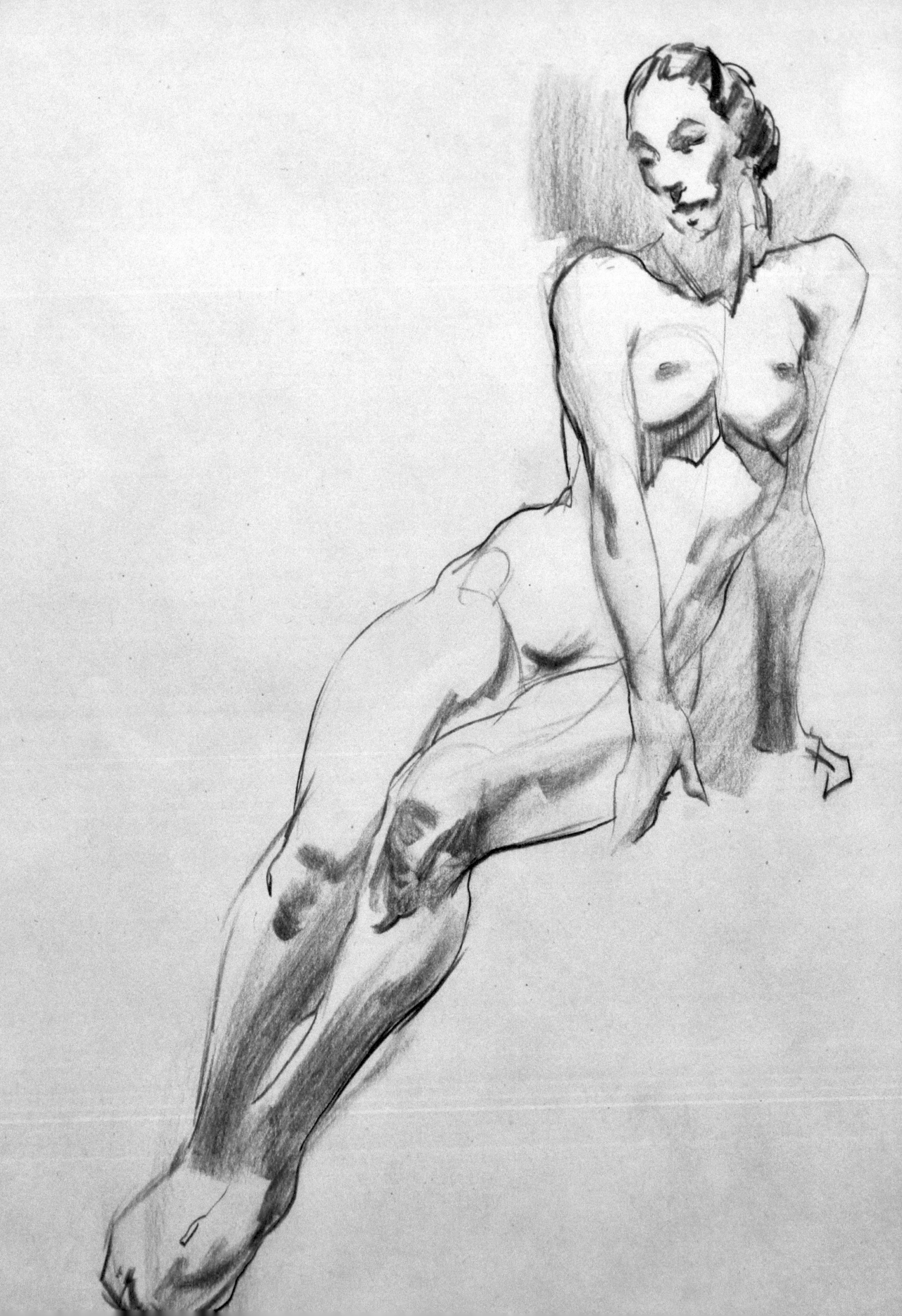

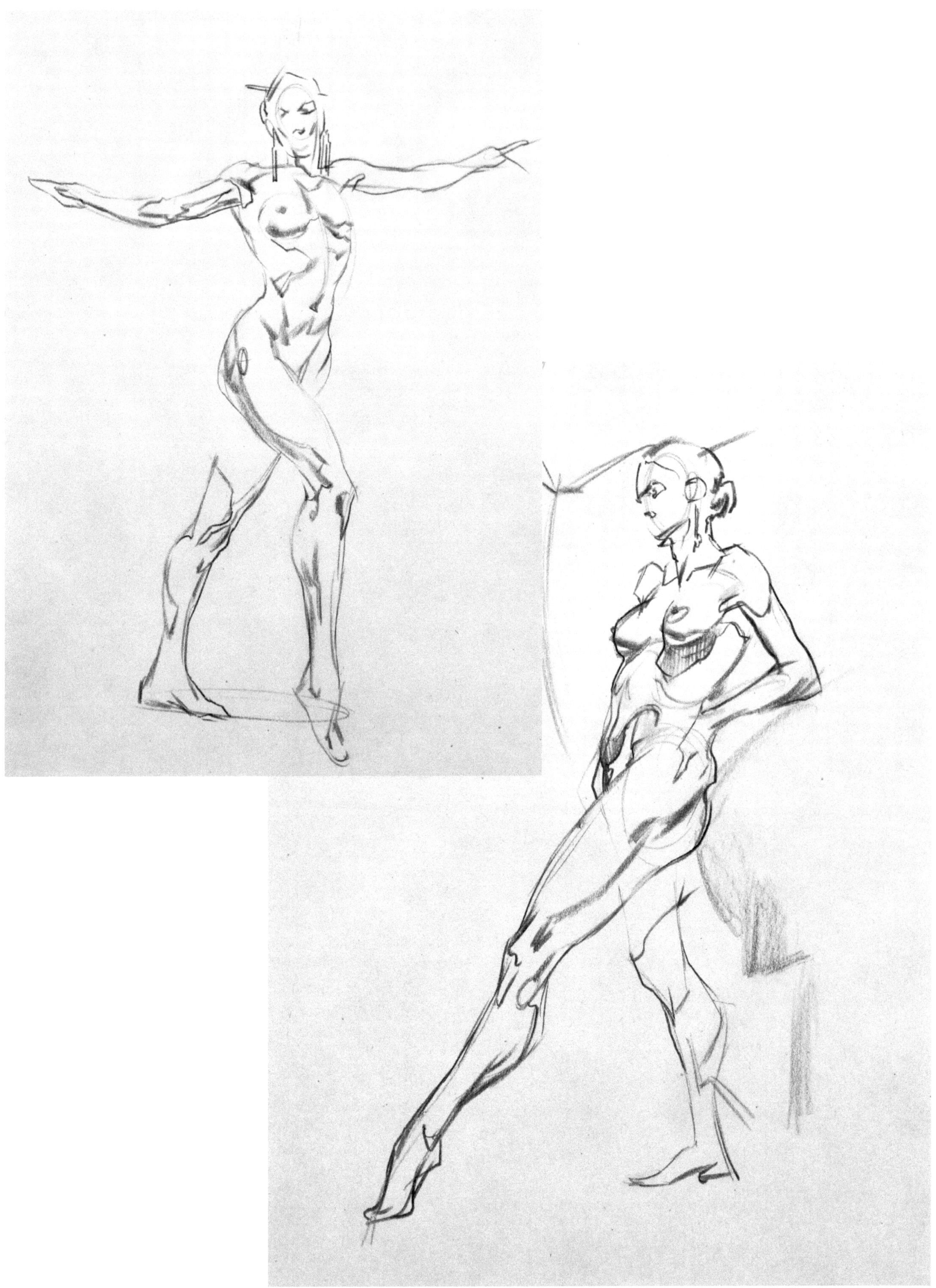

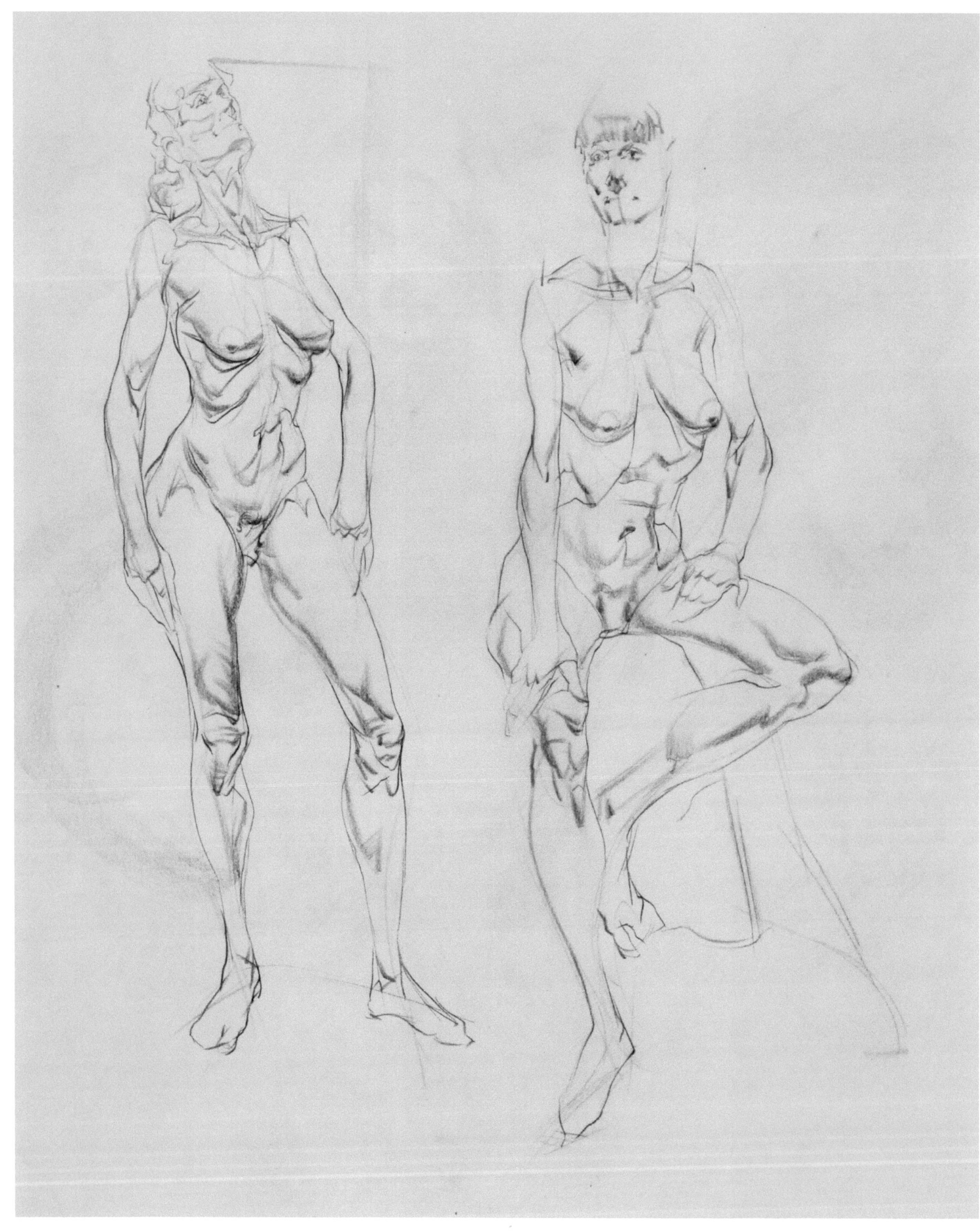

18x24
Charcoal/Newsprint
Quicksketch

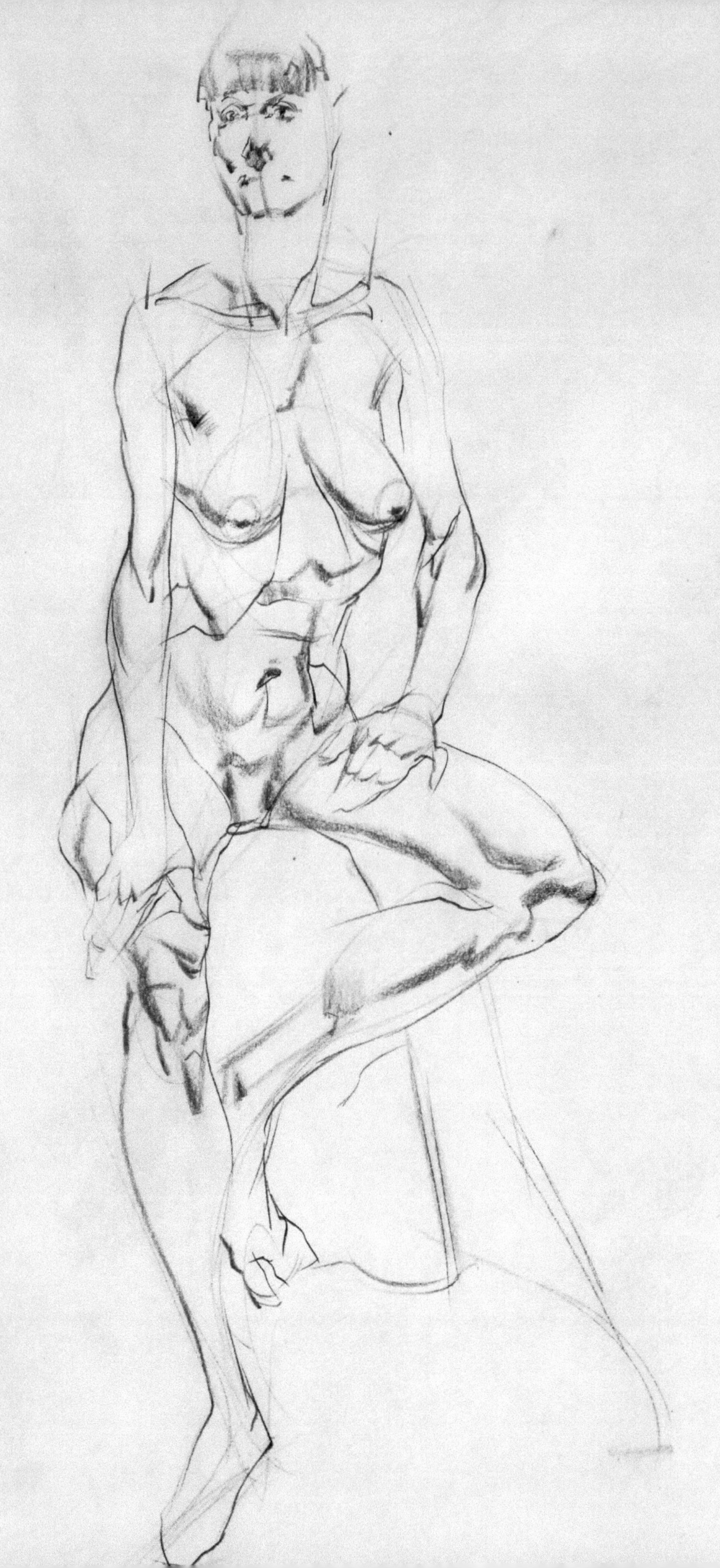

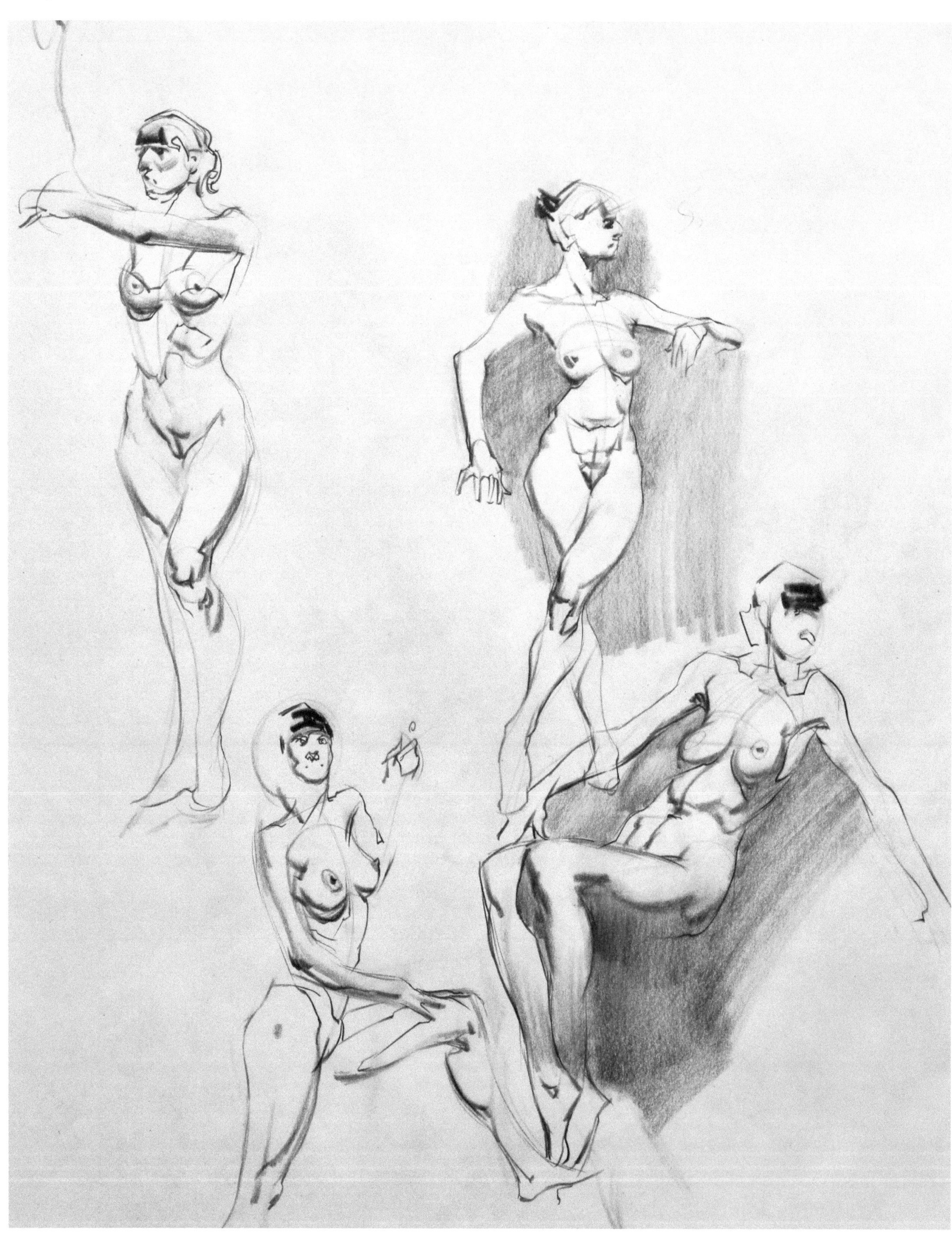

18x24
Charcoal/Newsprint
Quicksketch

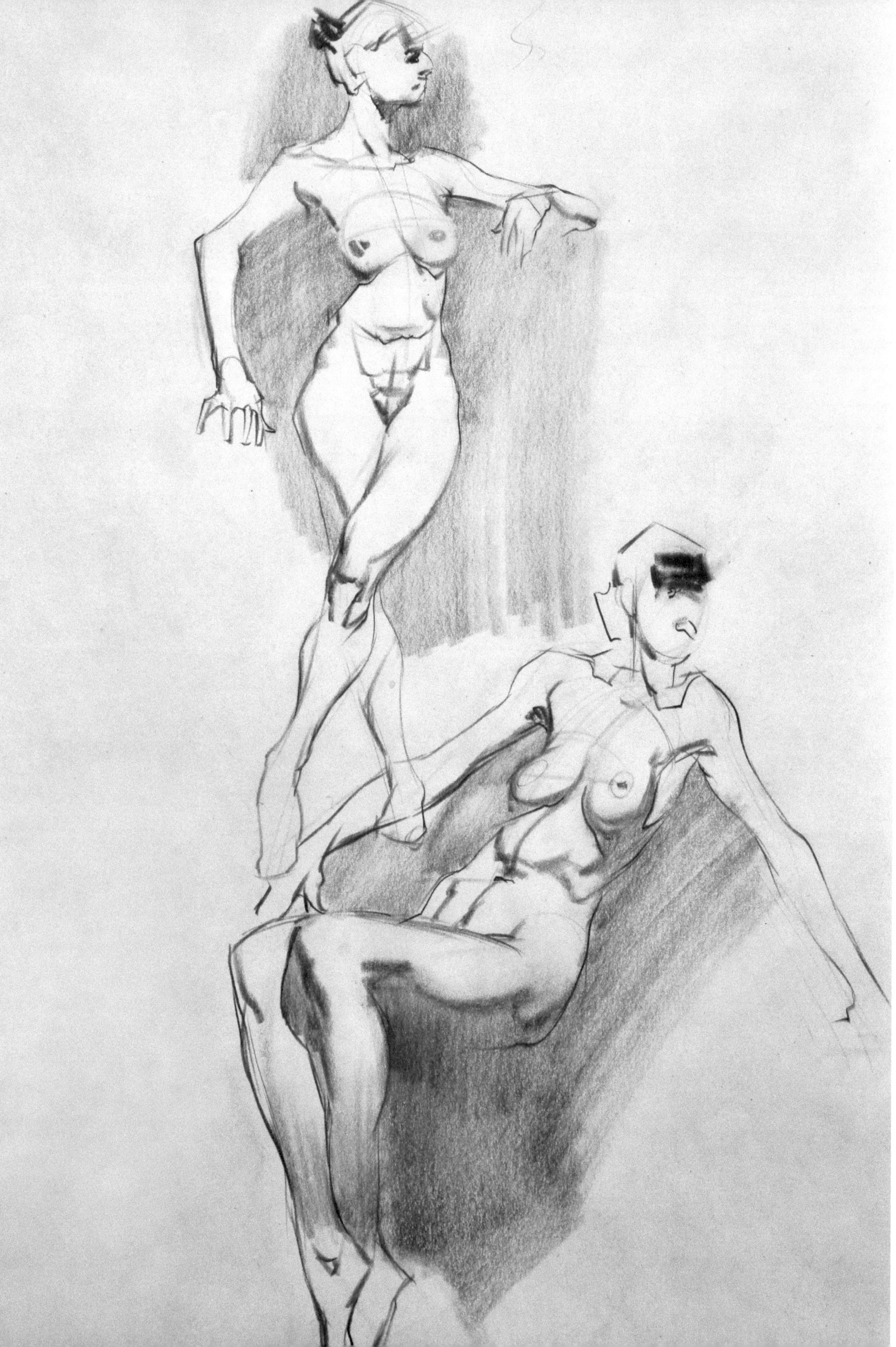

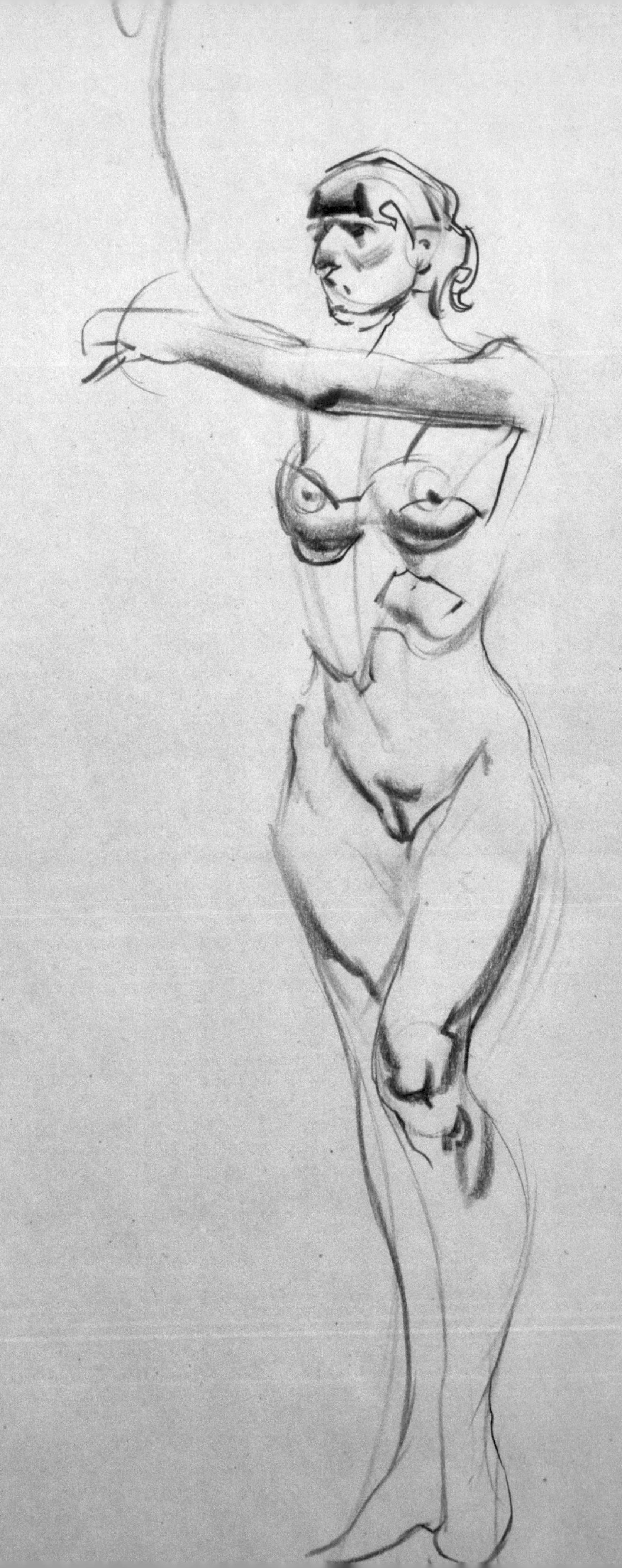

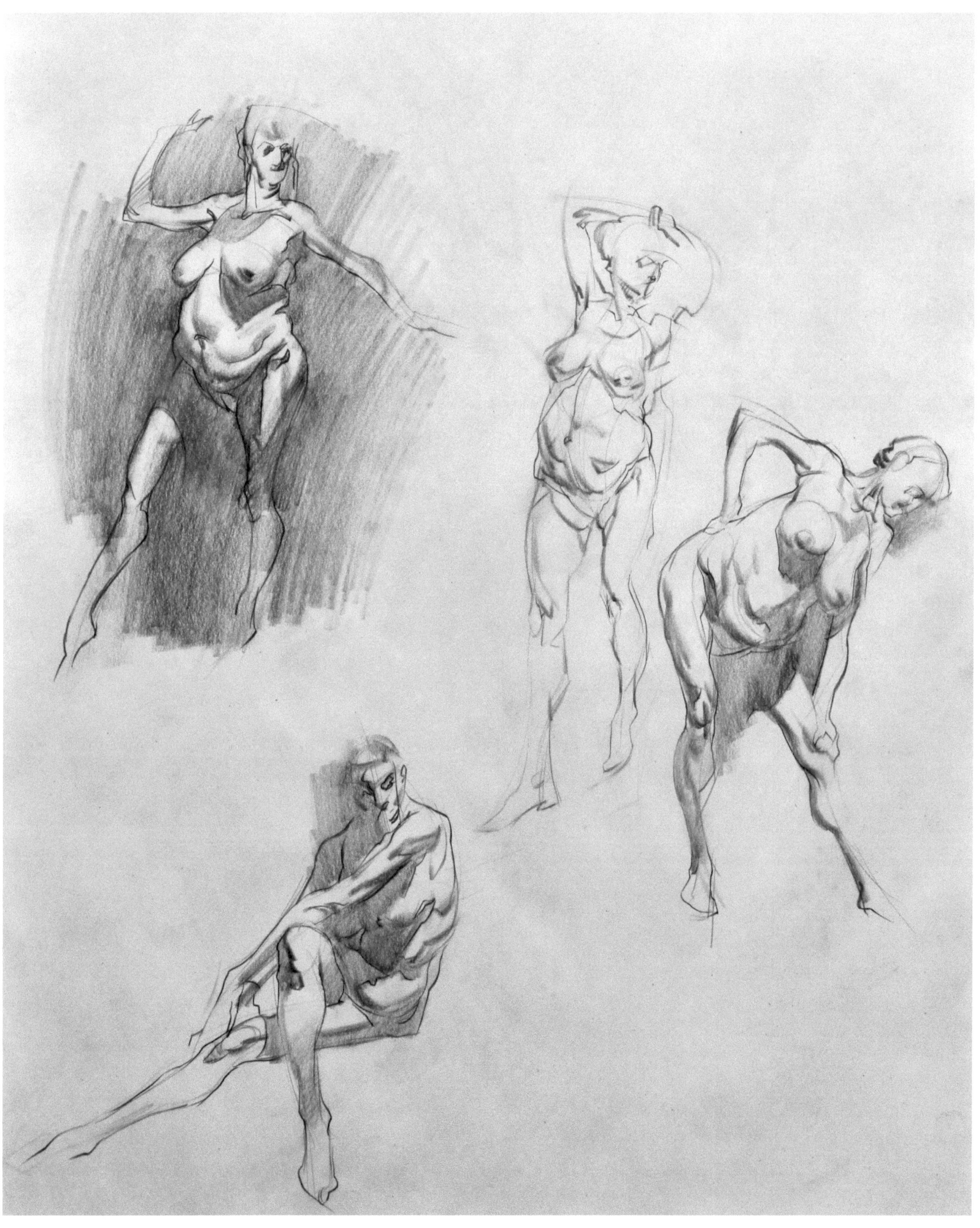

18x24
Charcoal/Newsprint
Quicksketch

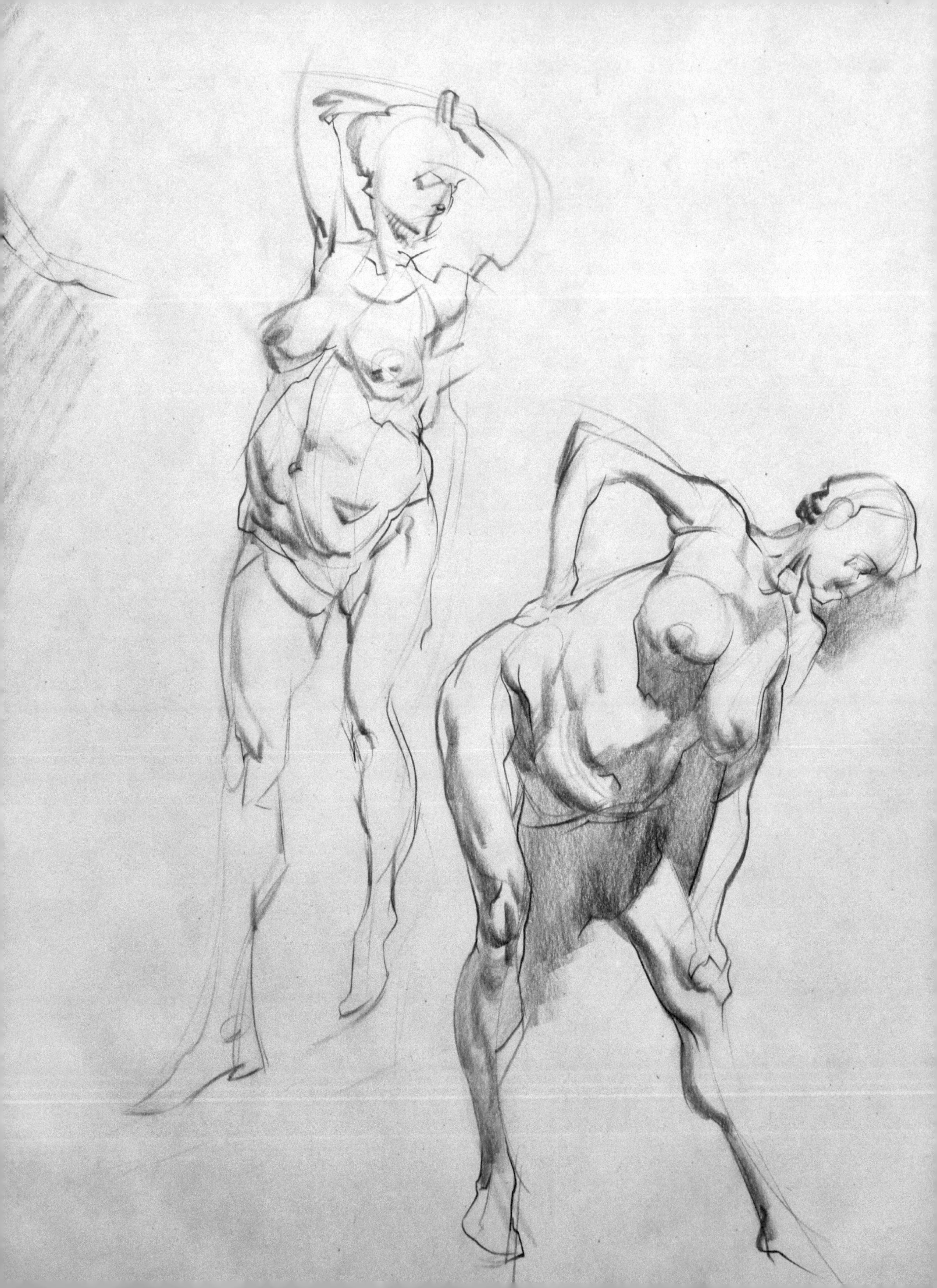

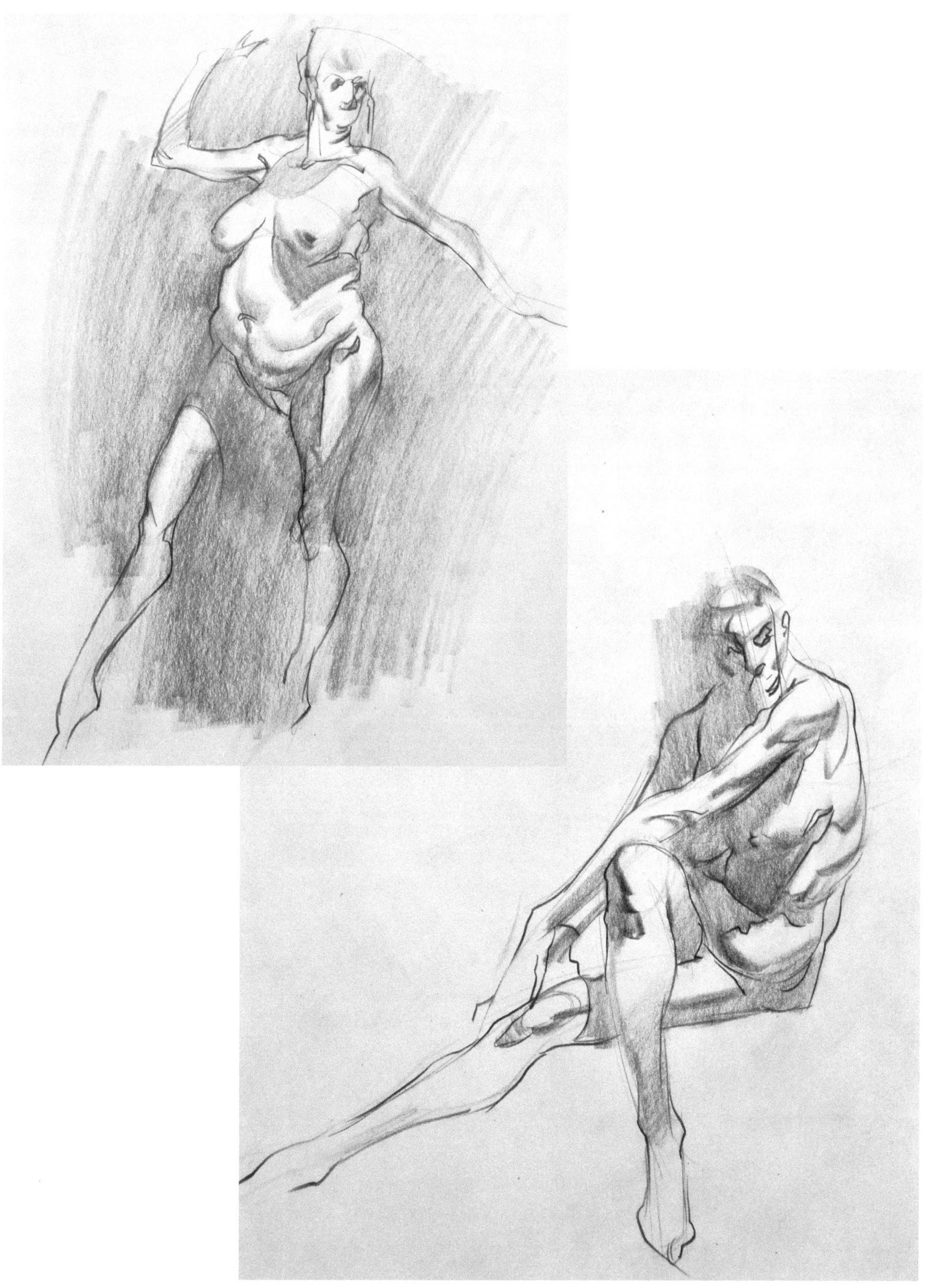

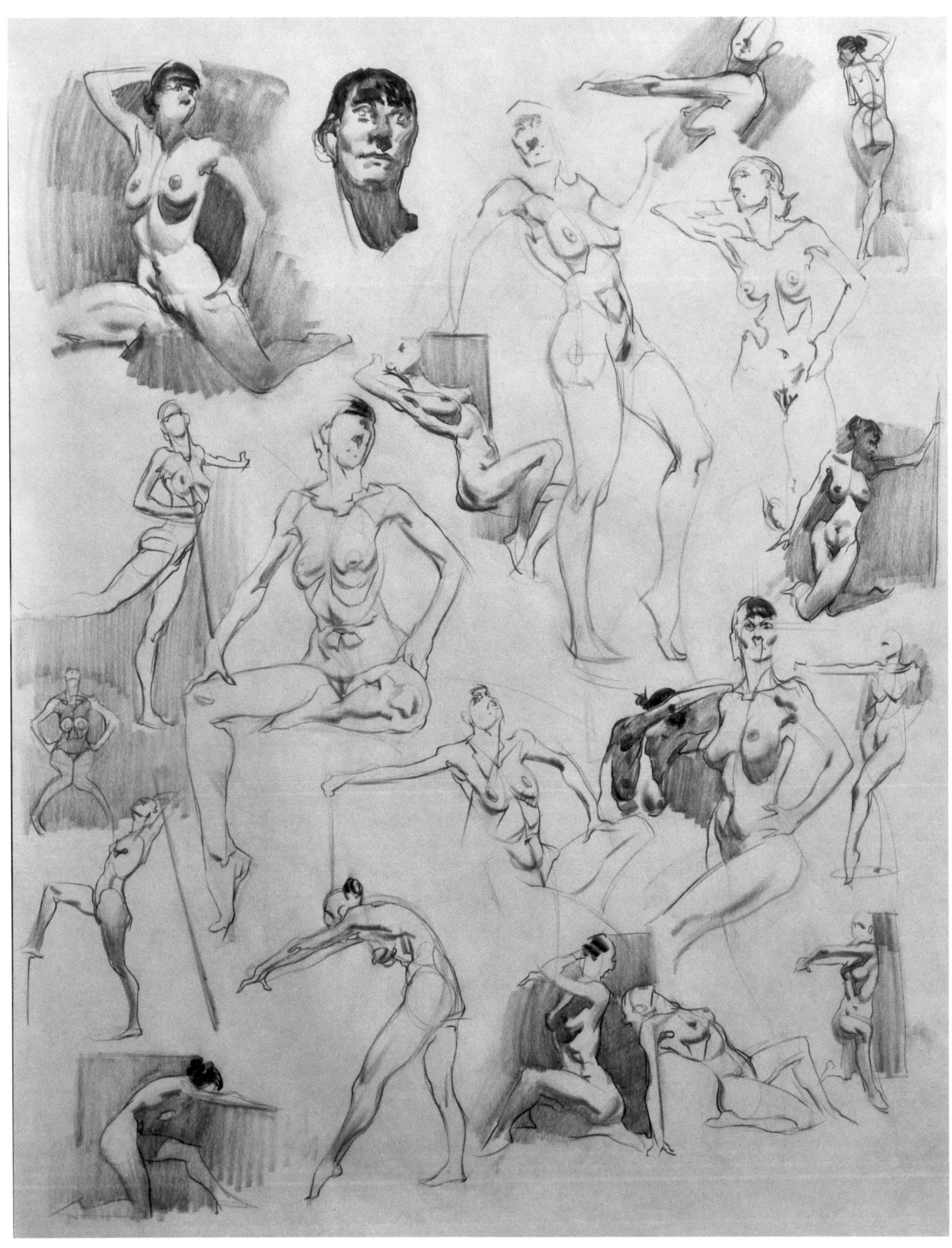

18x24
Charcoal/Newsprint
Quicksketch

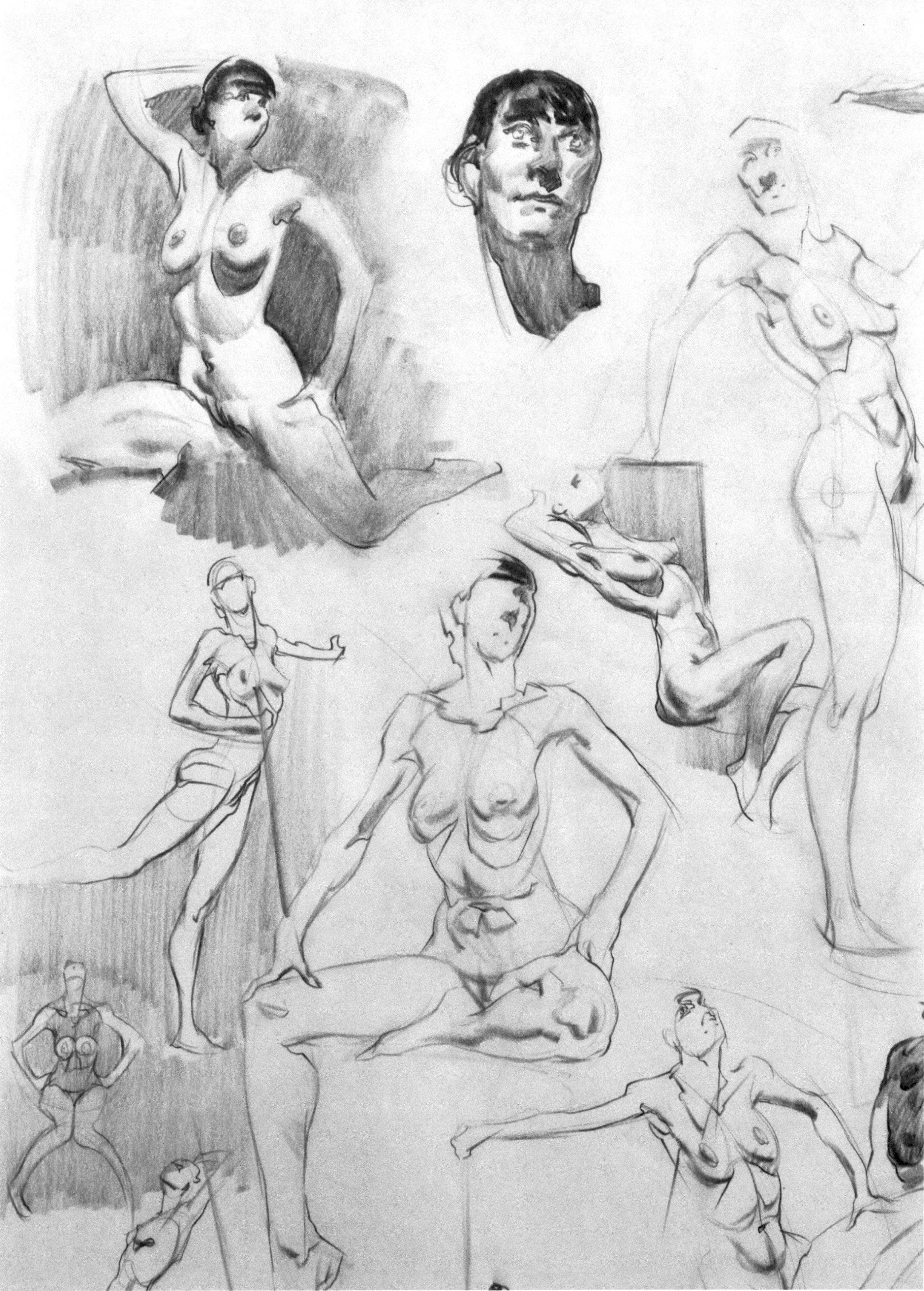

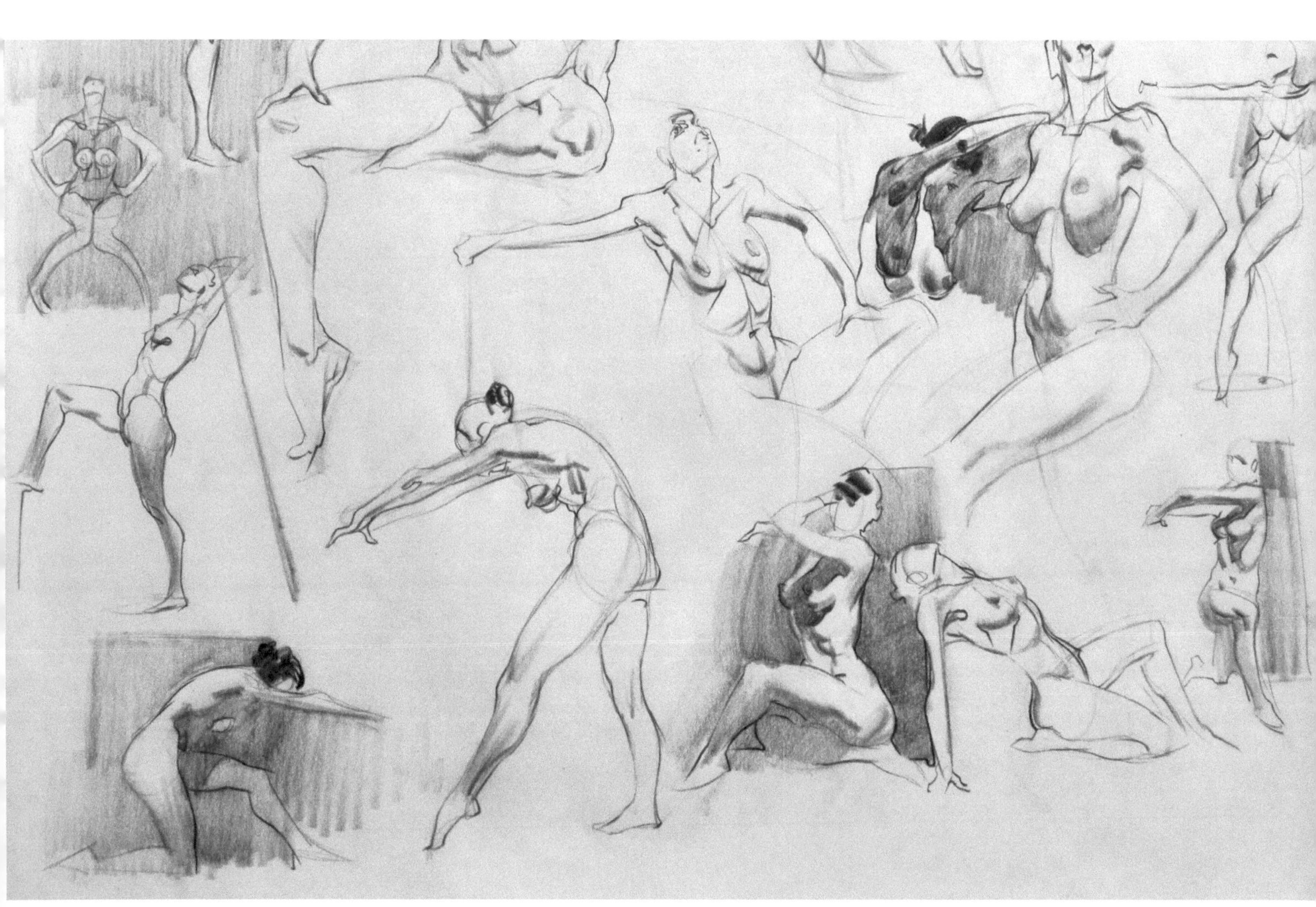

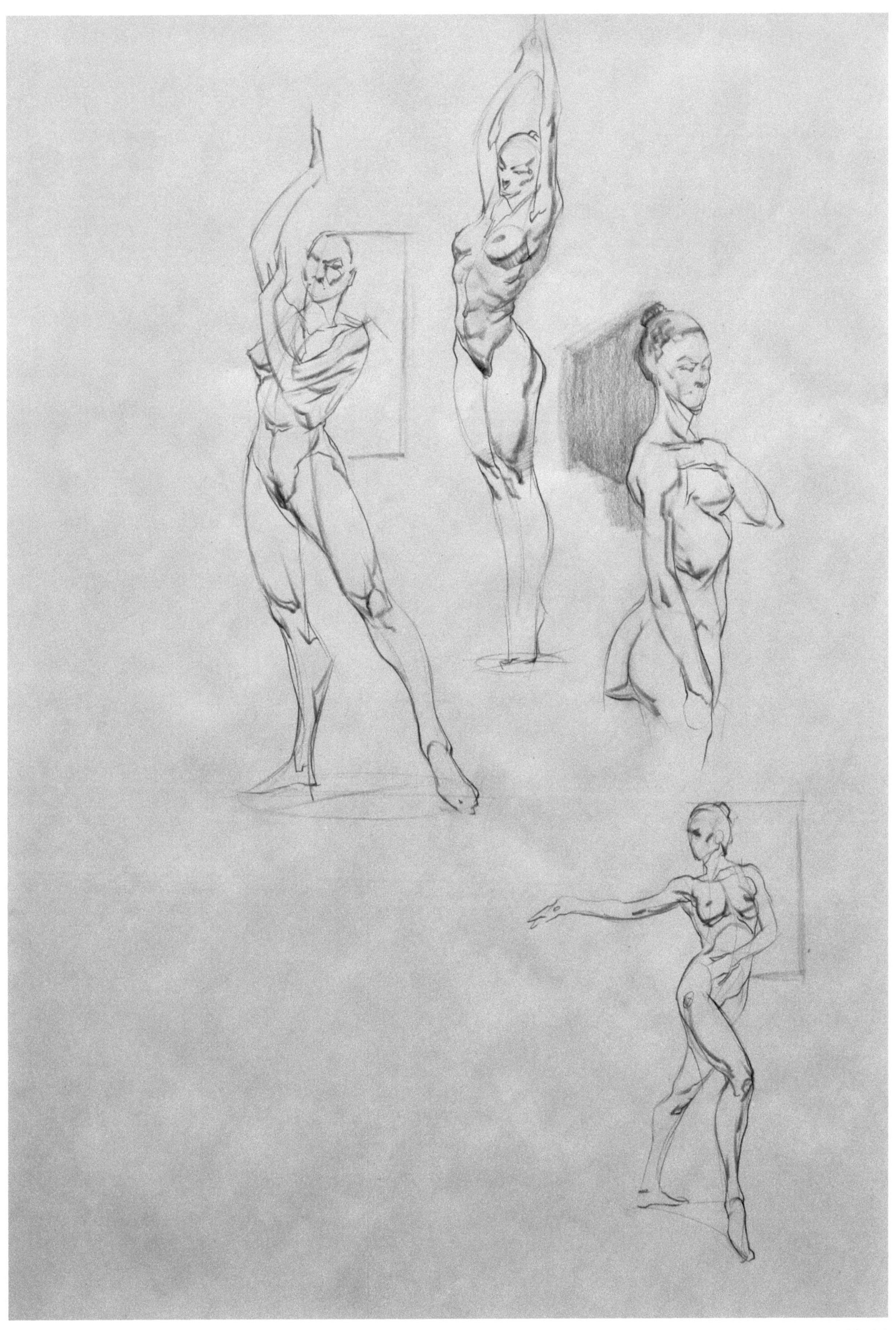

18x24
Charcoal/Newsprint
Quicksketch

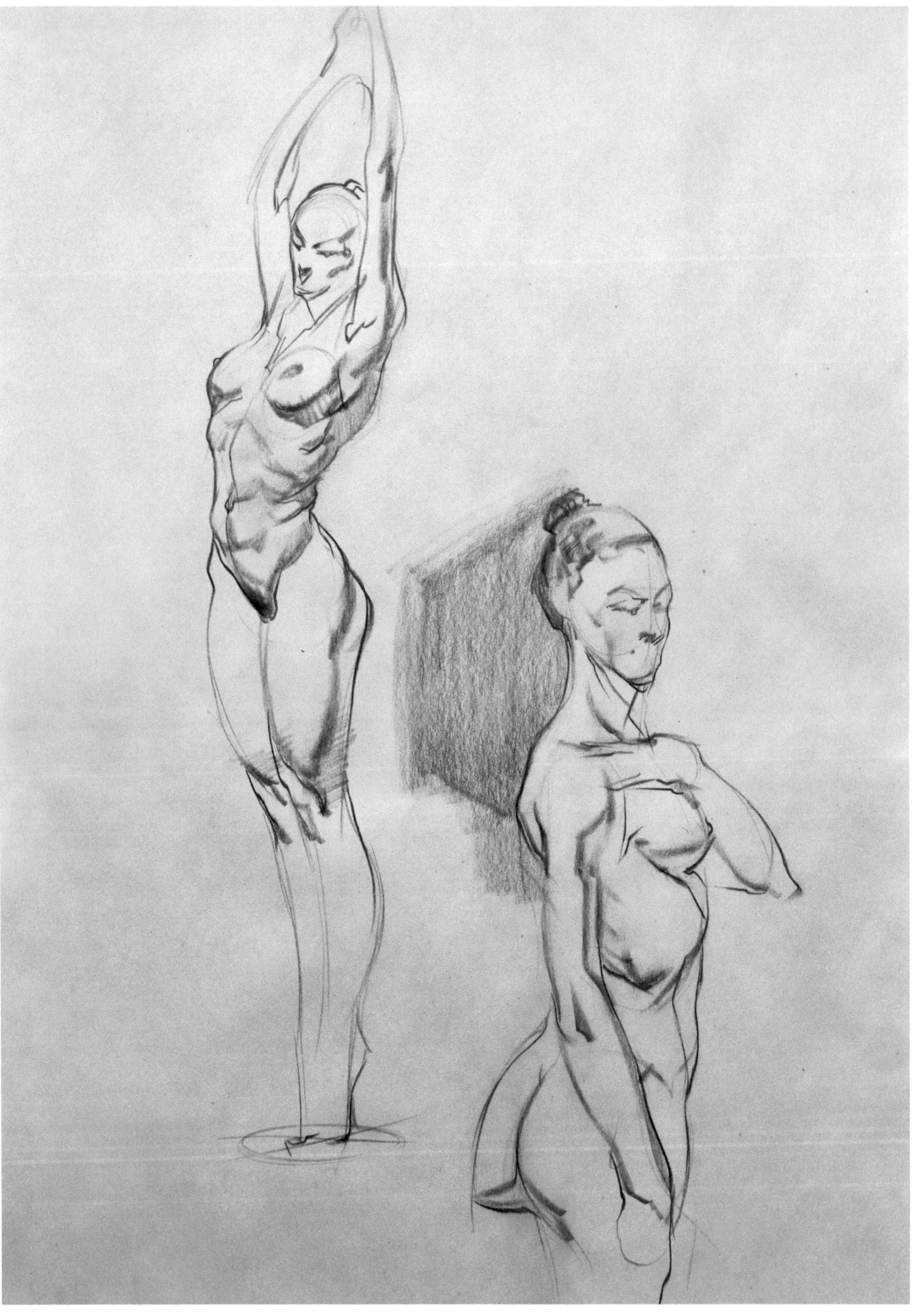

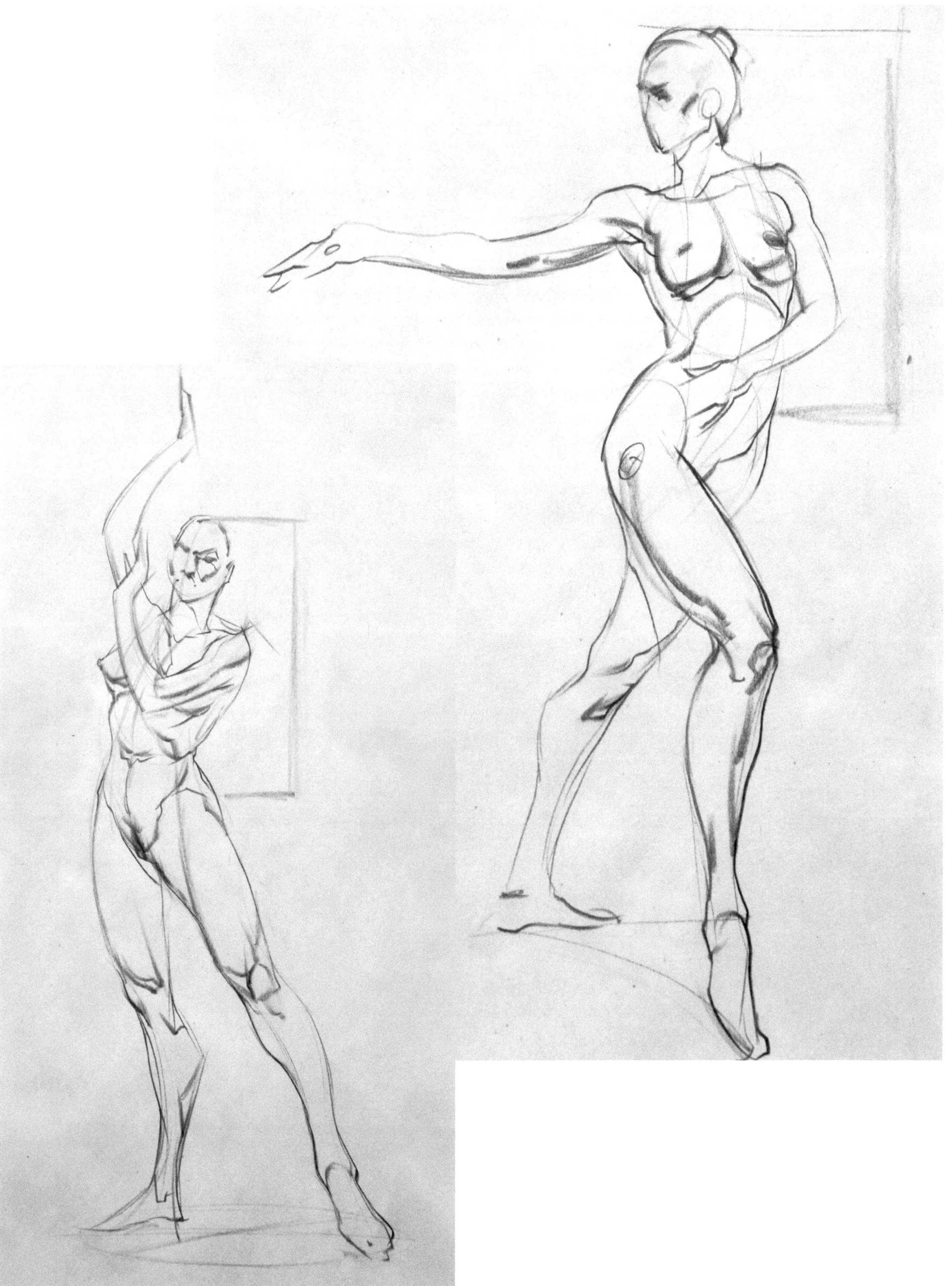

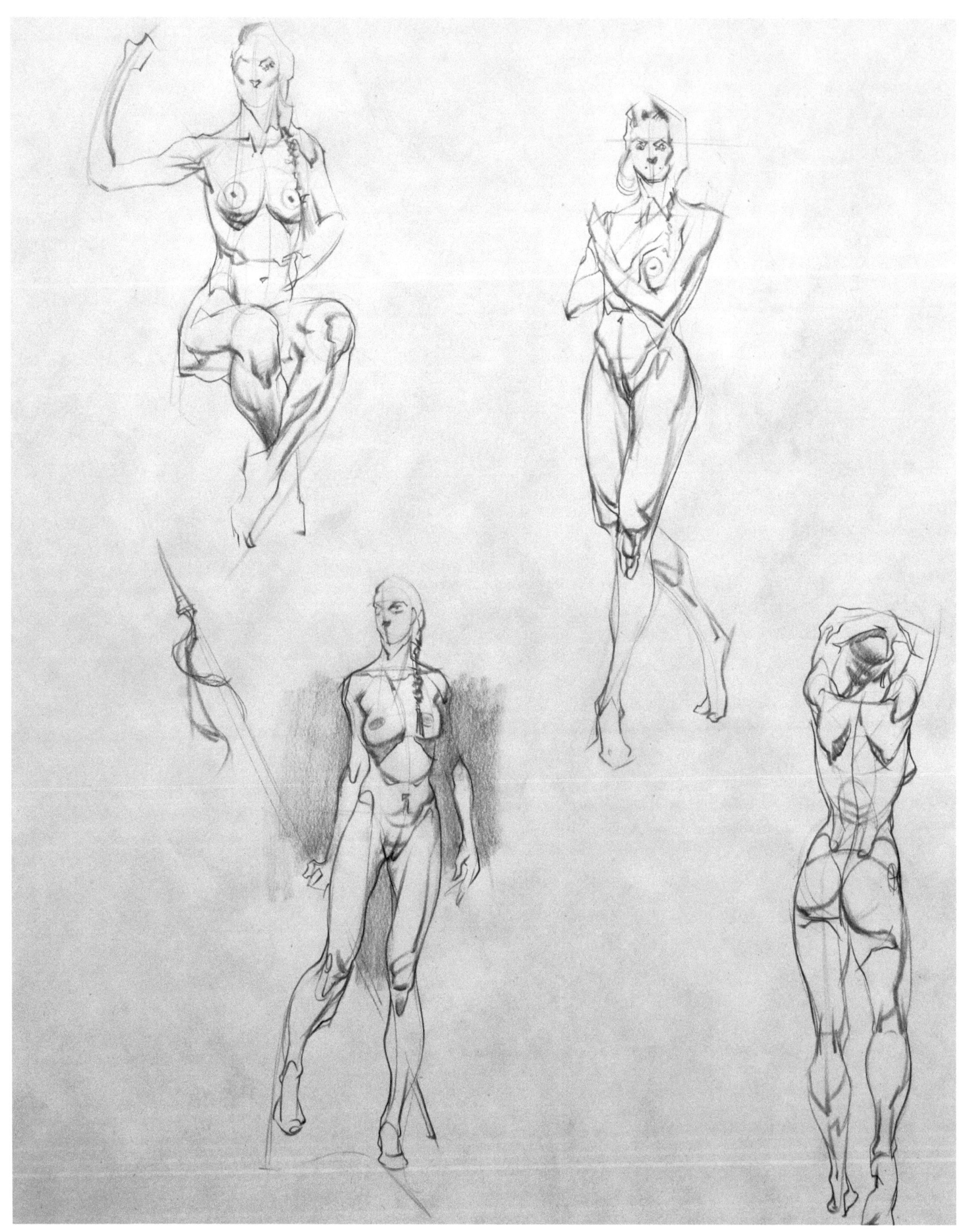

18x24
Charcoal/Newsprint
Quicksketch

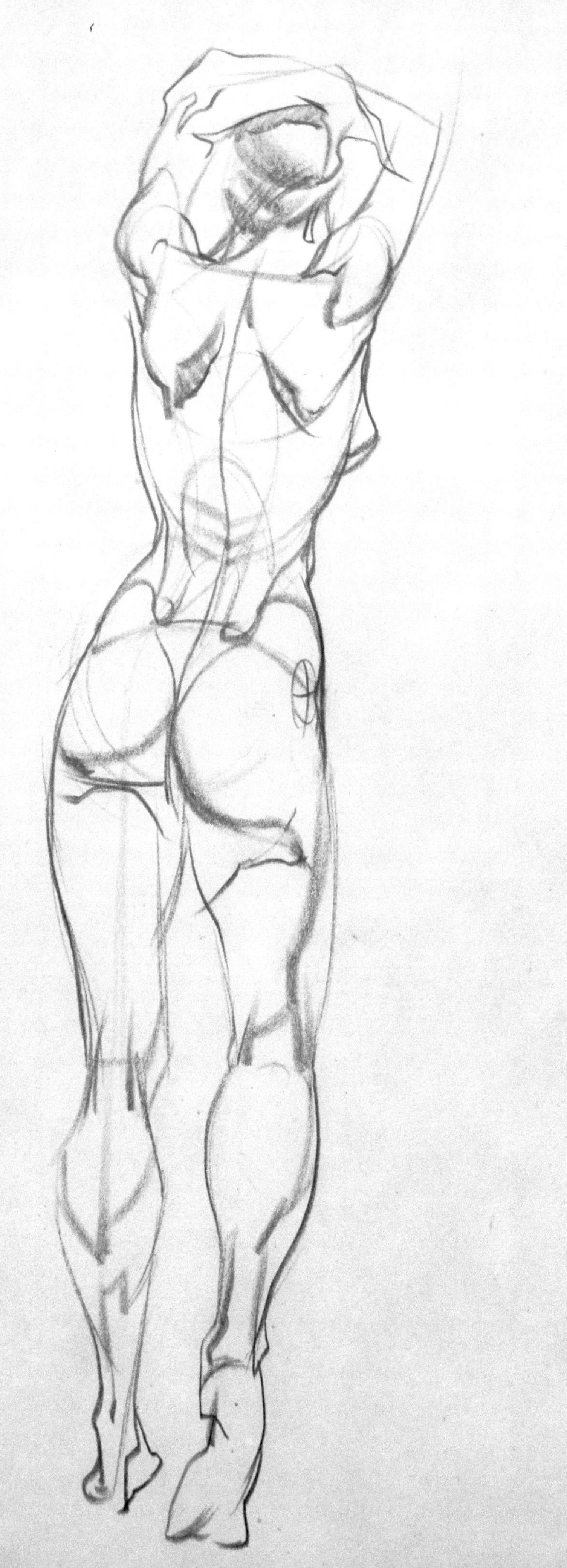

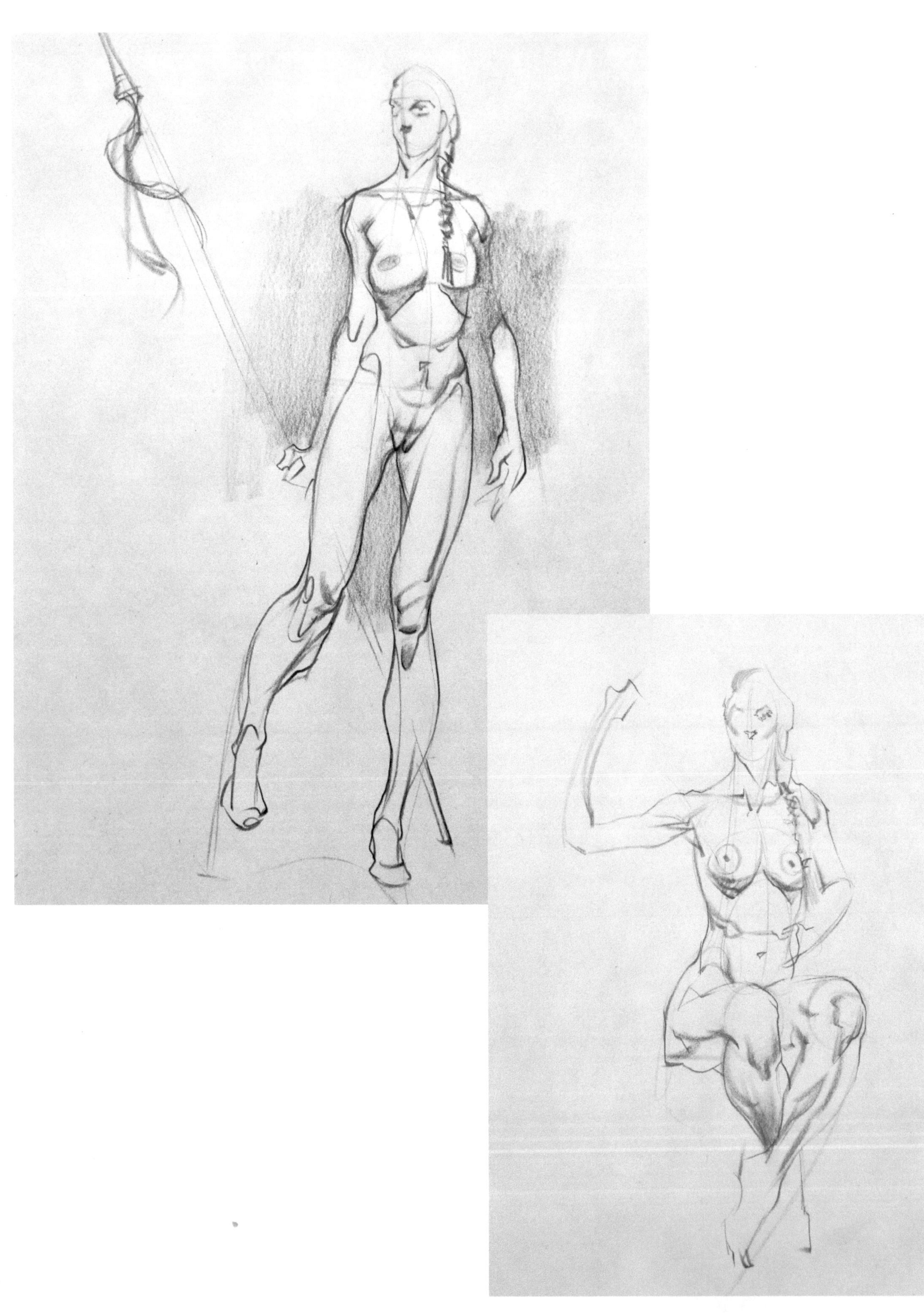

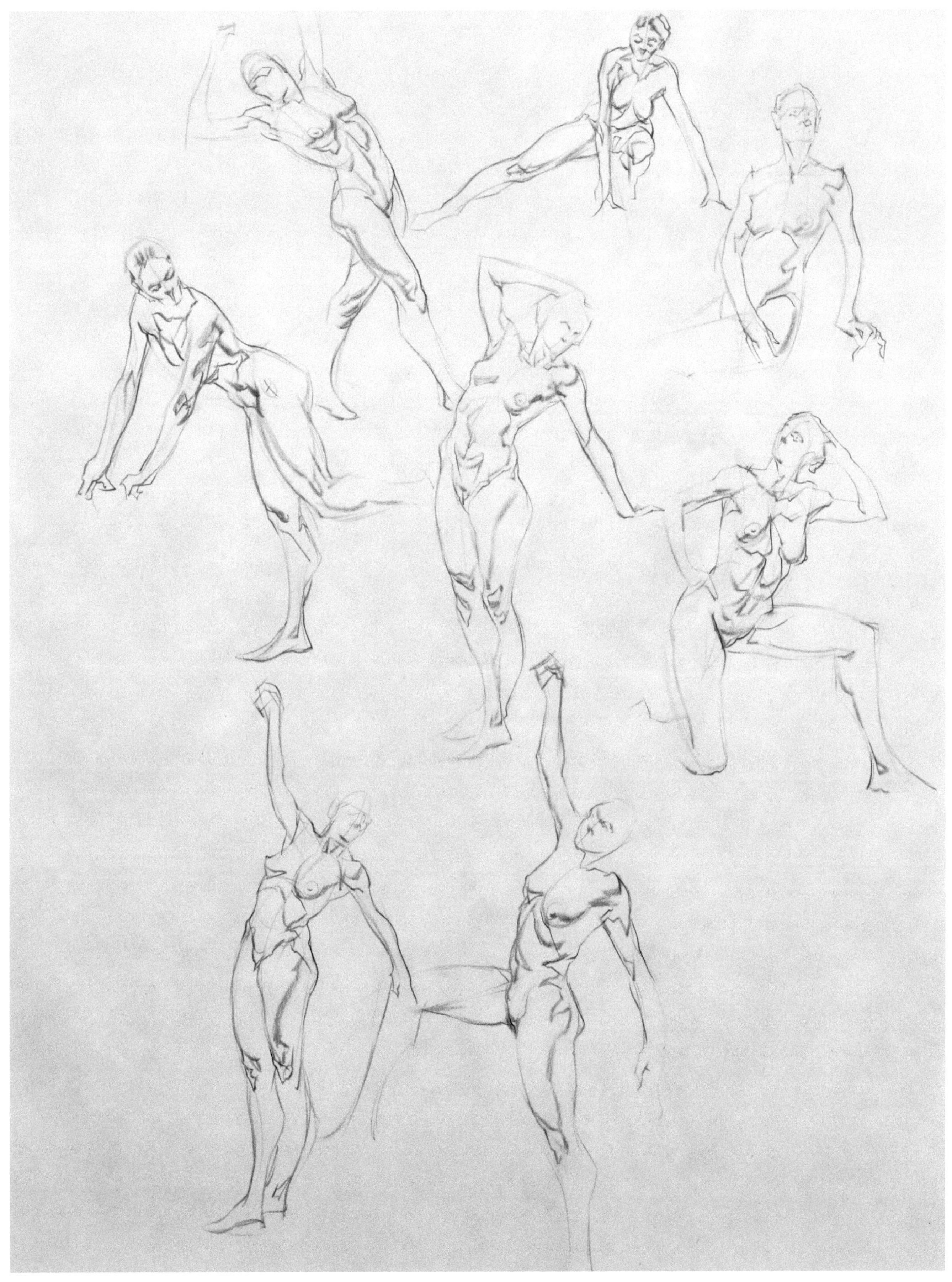

18x24
Charcoal/Newsprint
Quicksketch

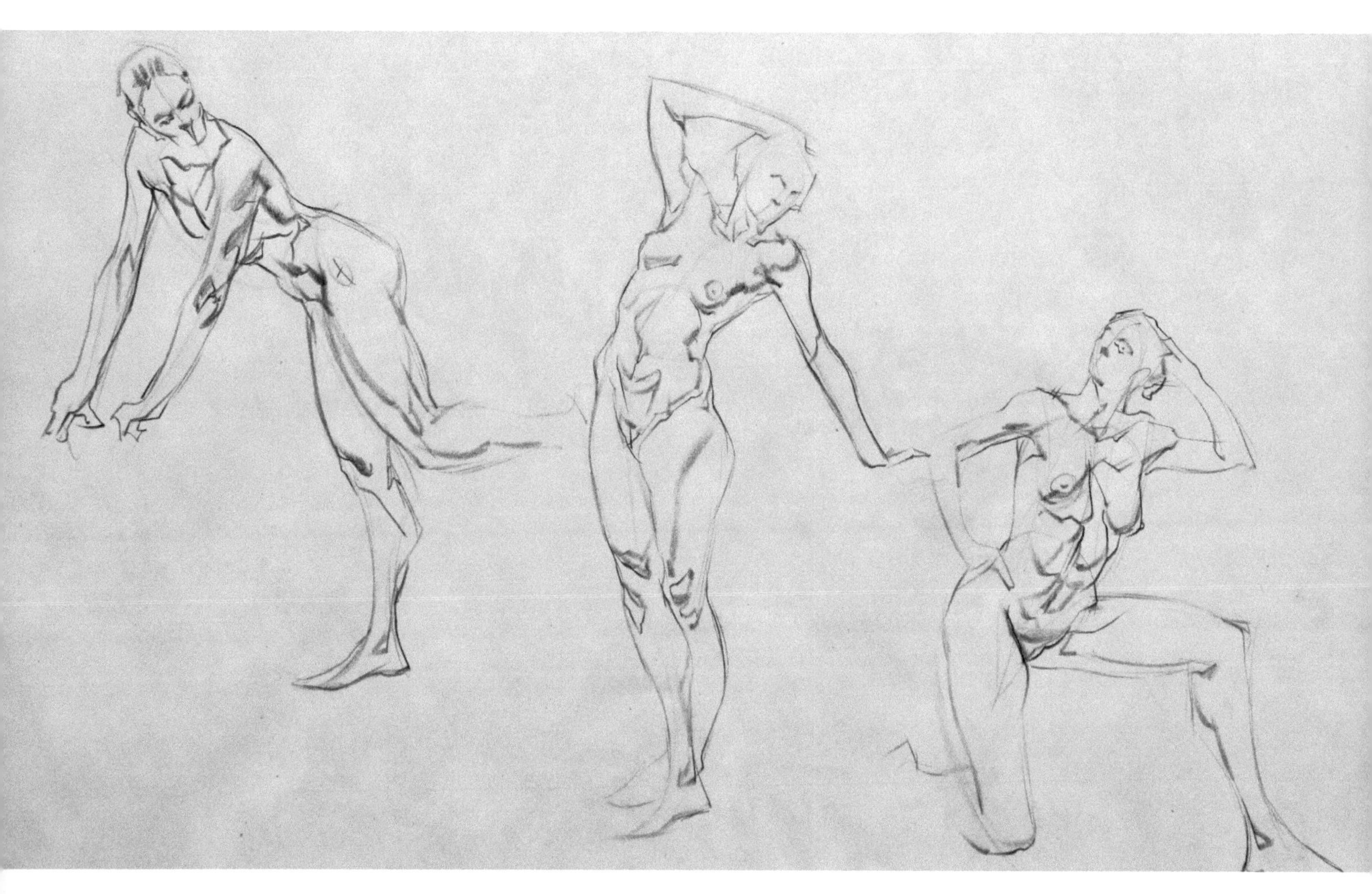

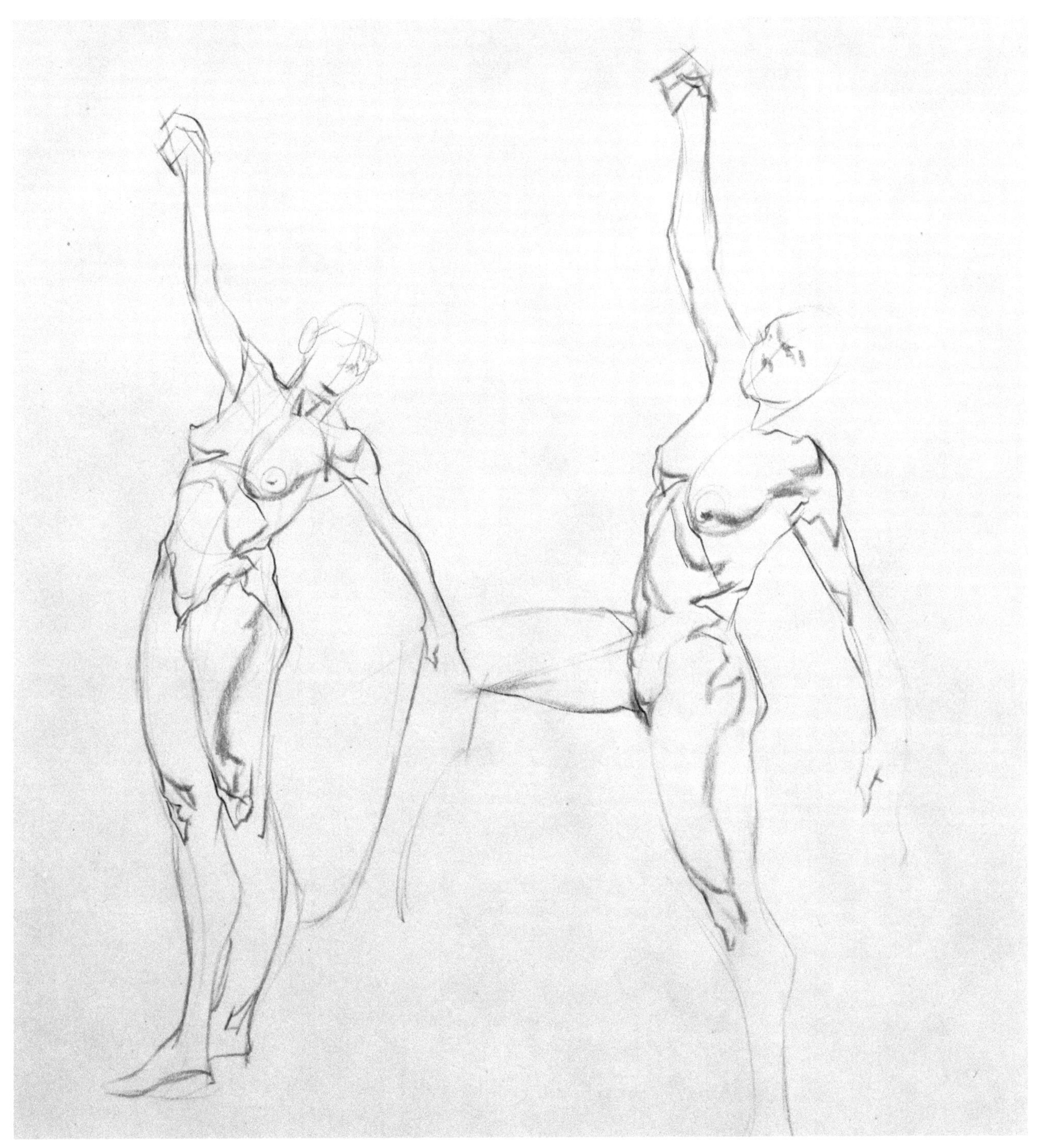

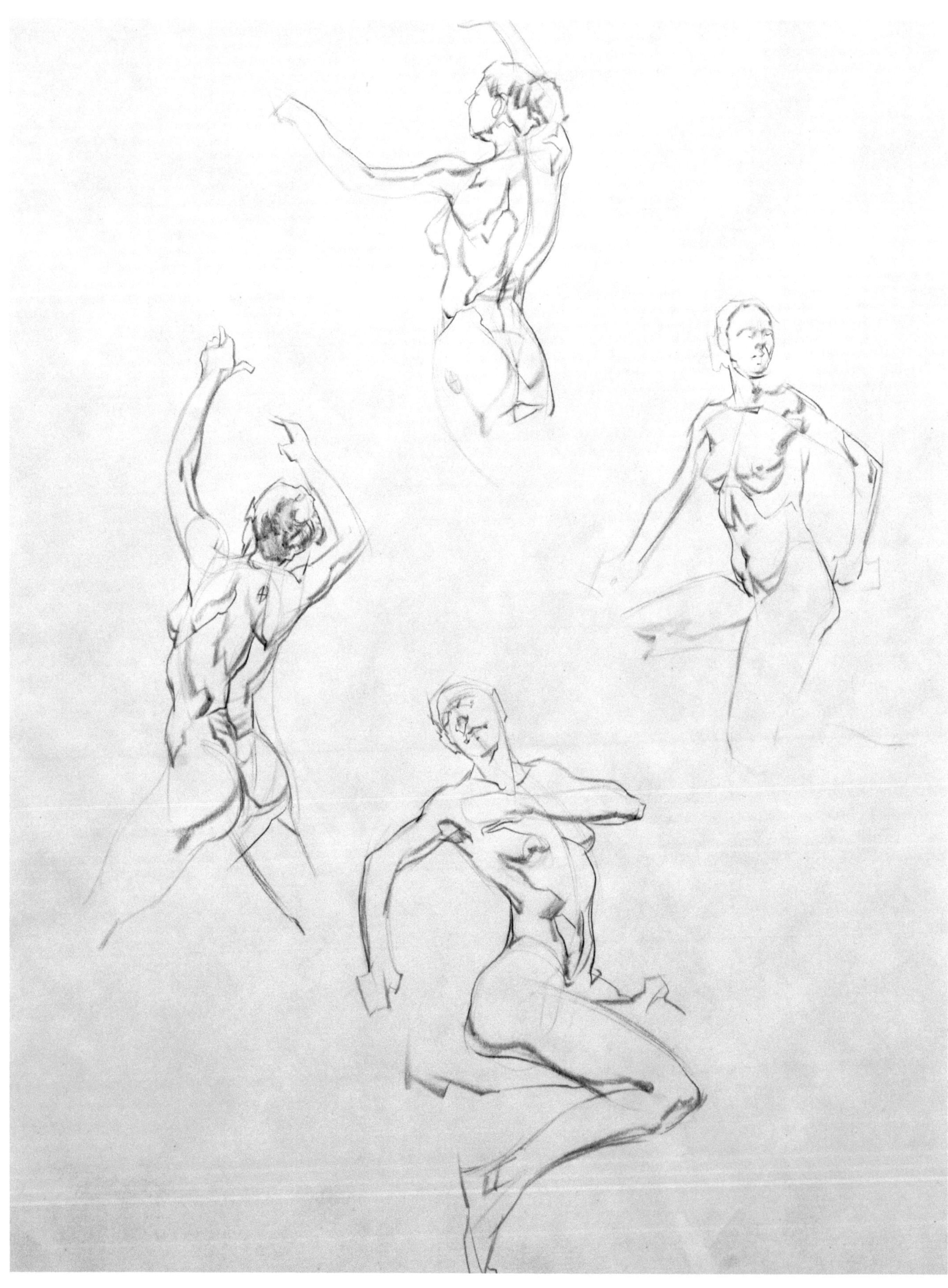

18x24
Charcoal/Newsprint
Quicksketch

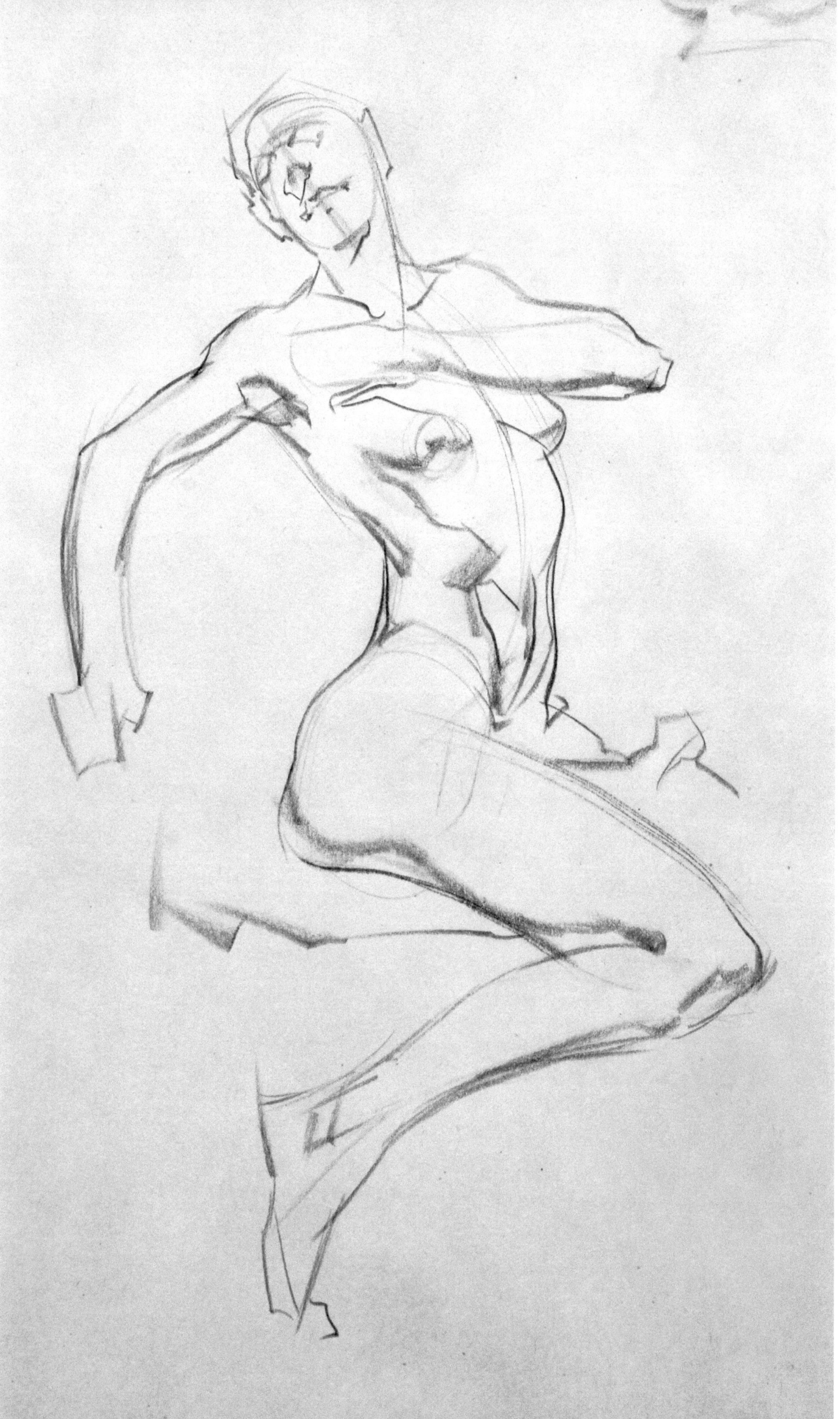

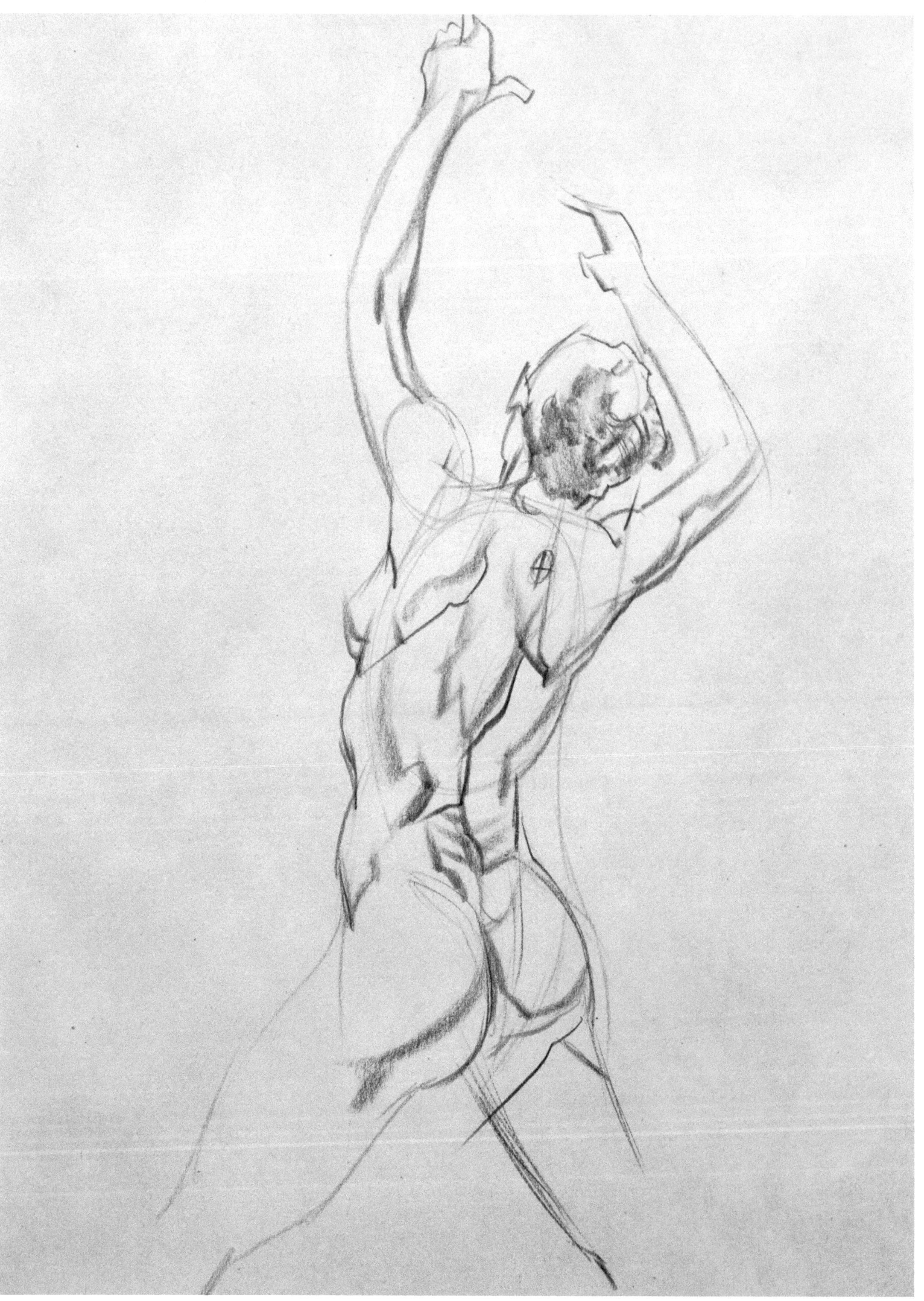

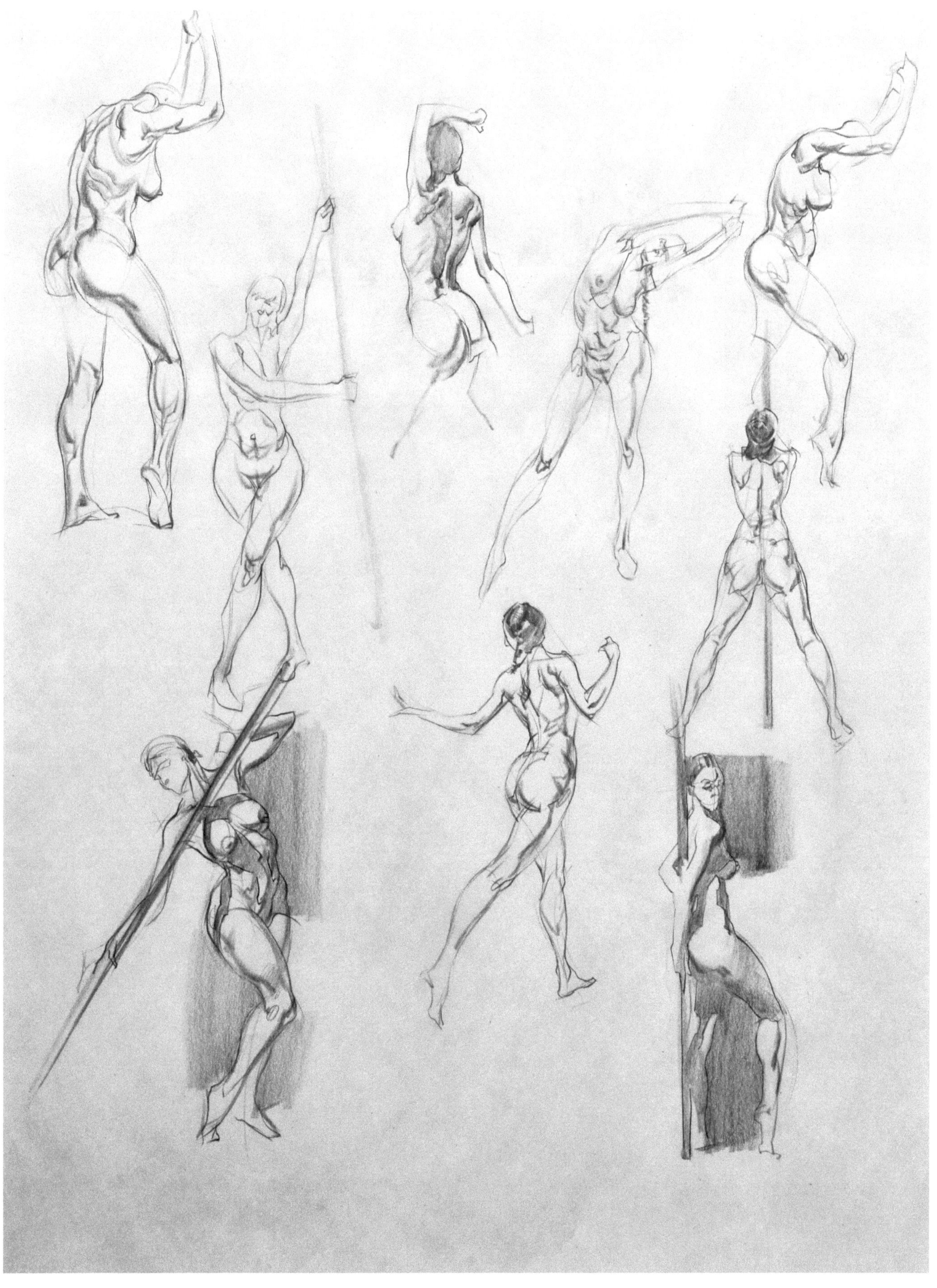

18x24
Charcoal/Newsprint
Quicksketch

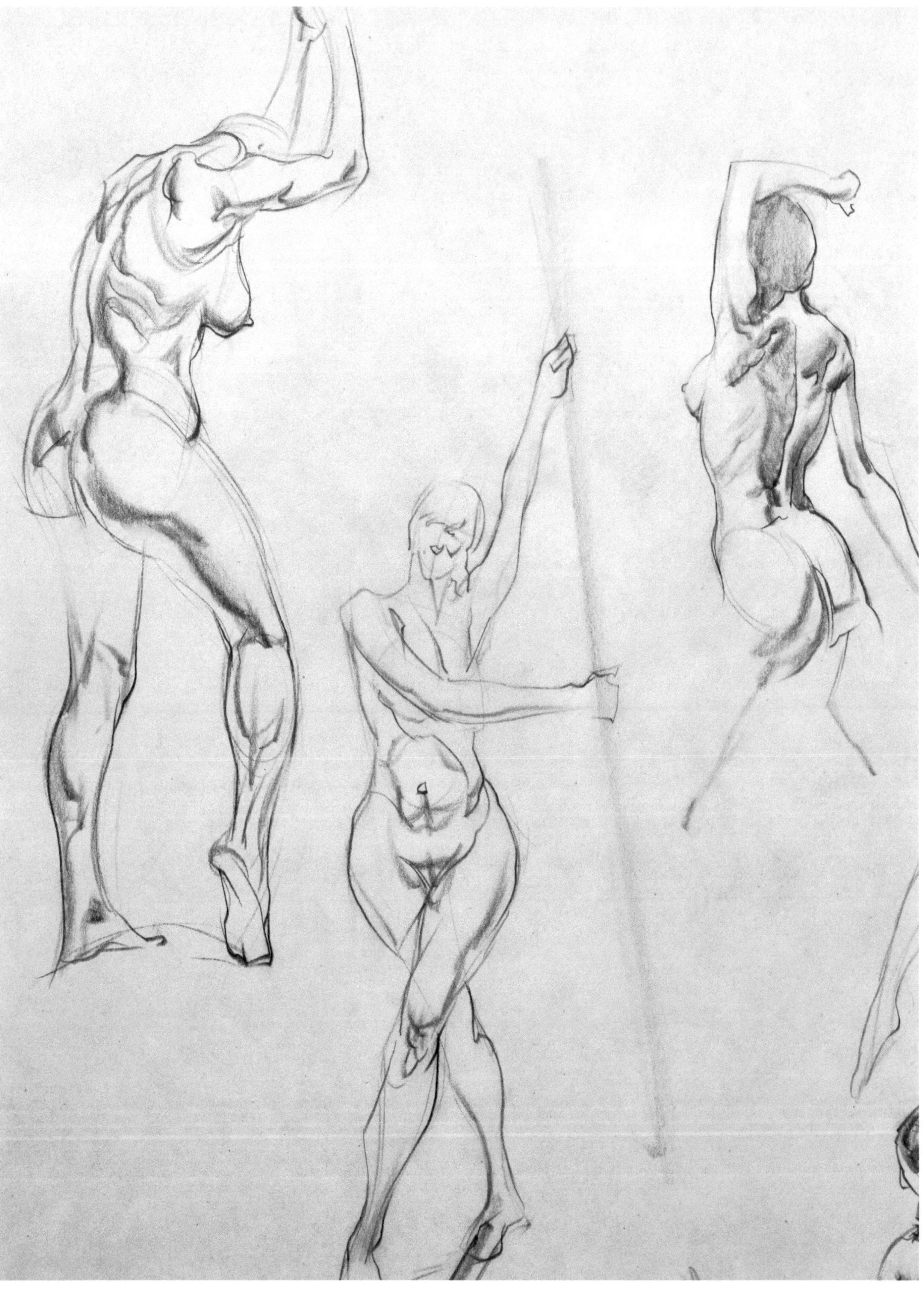

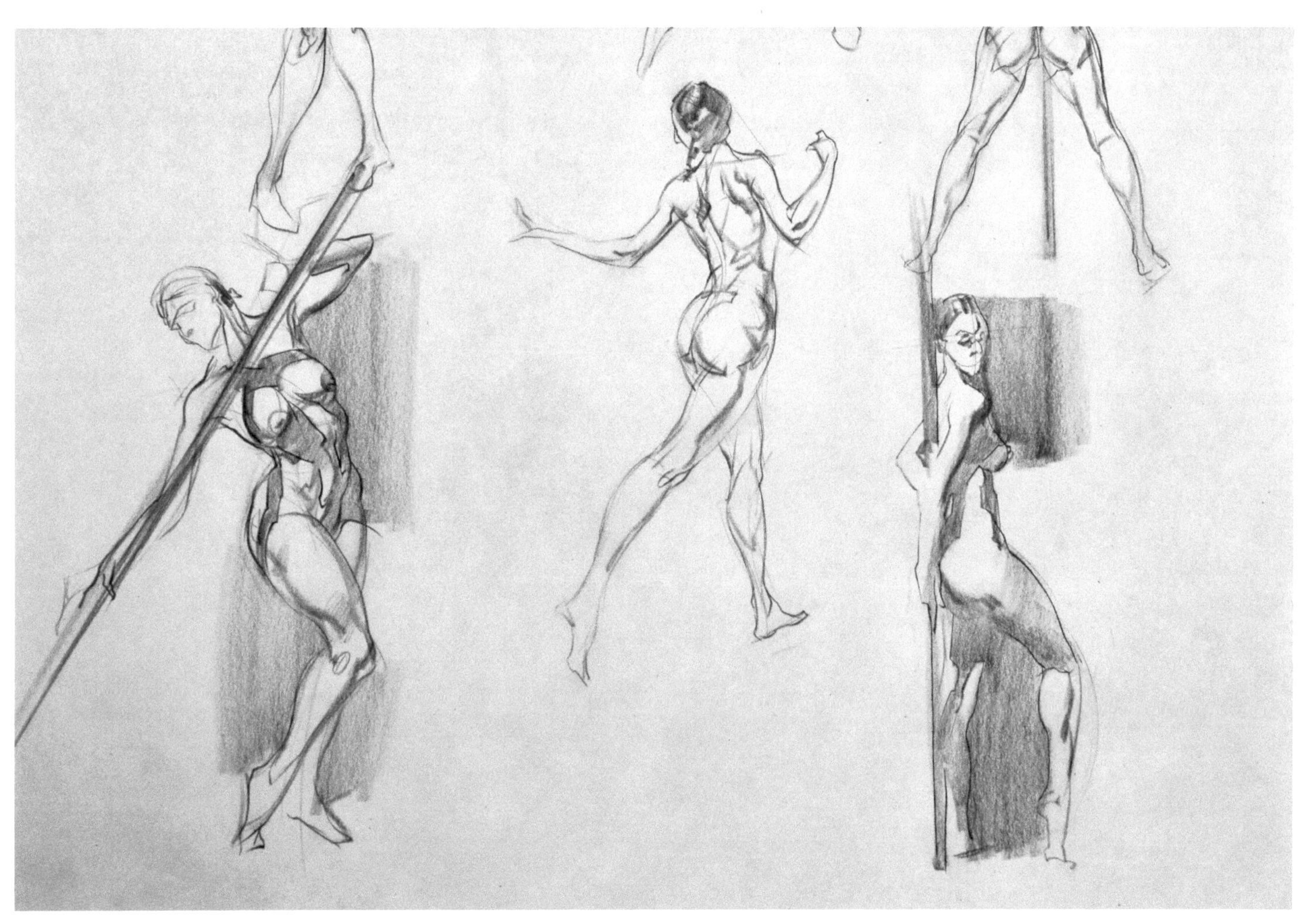

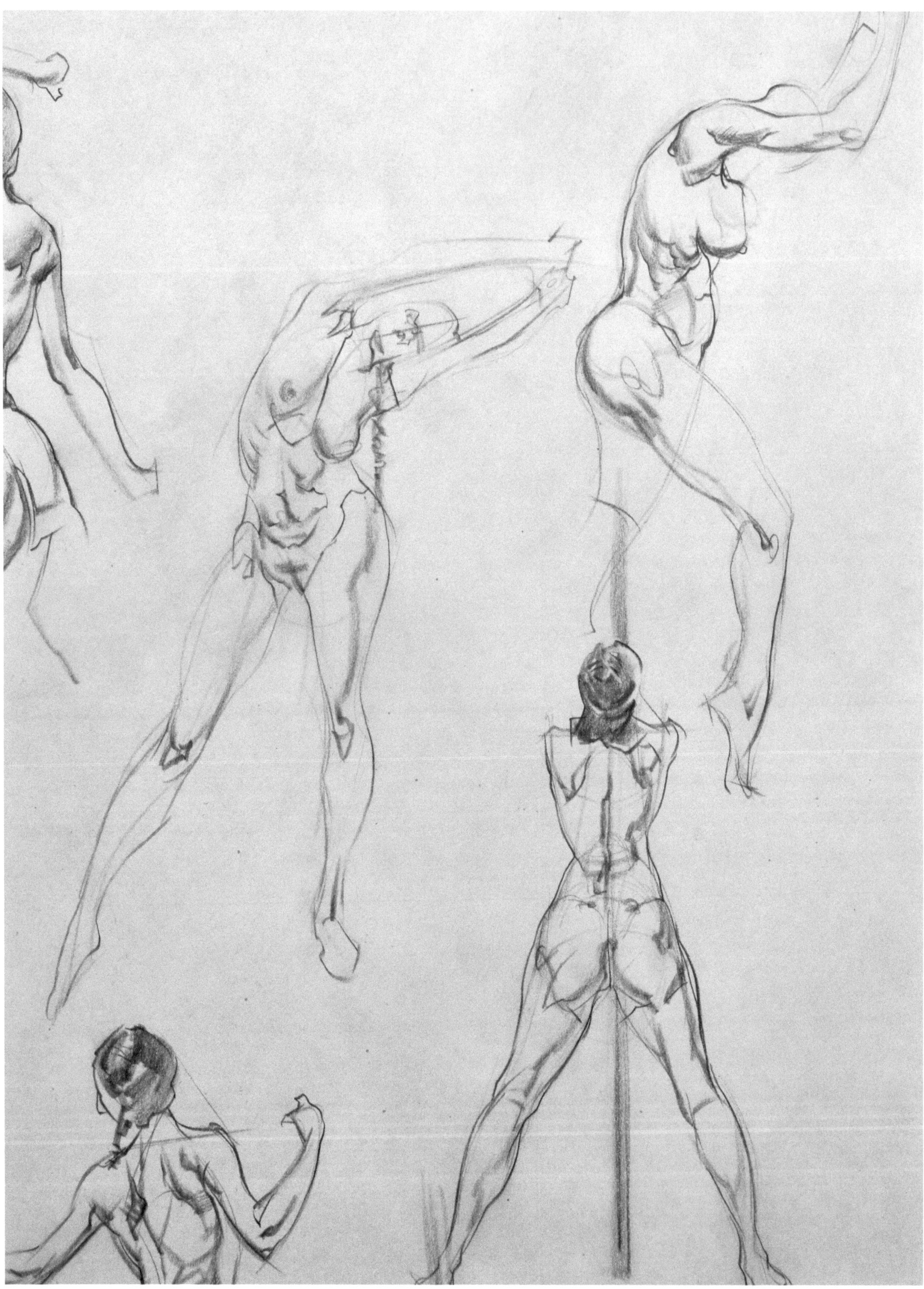

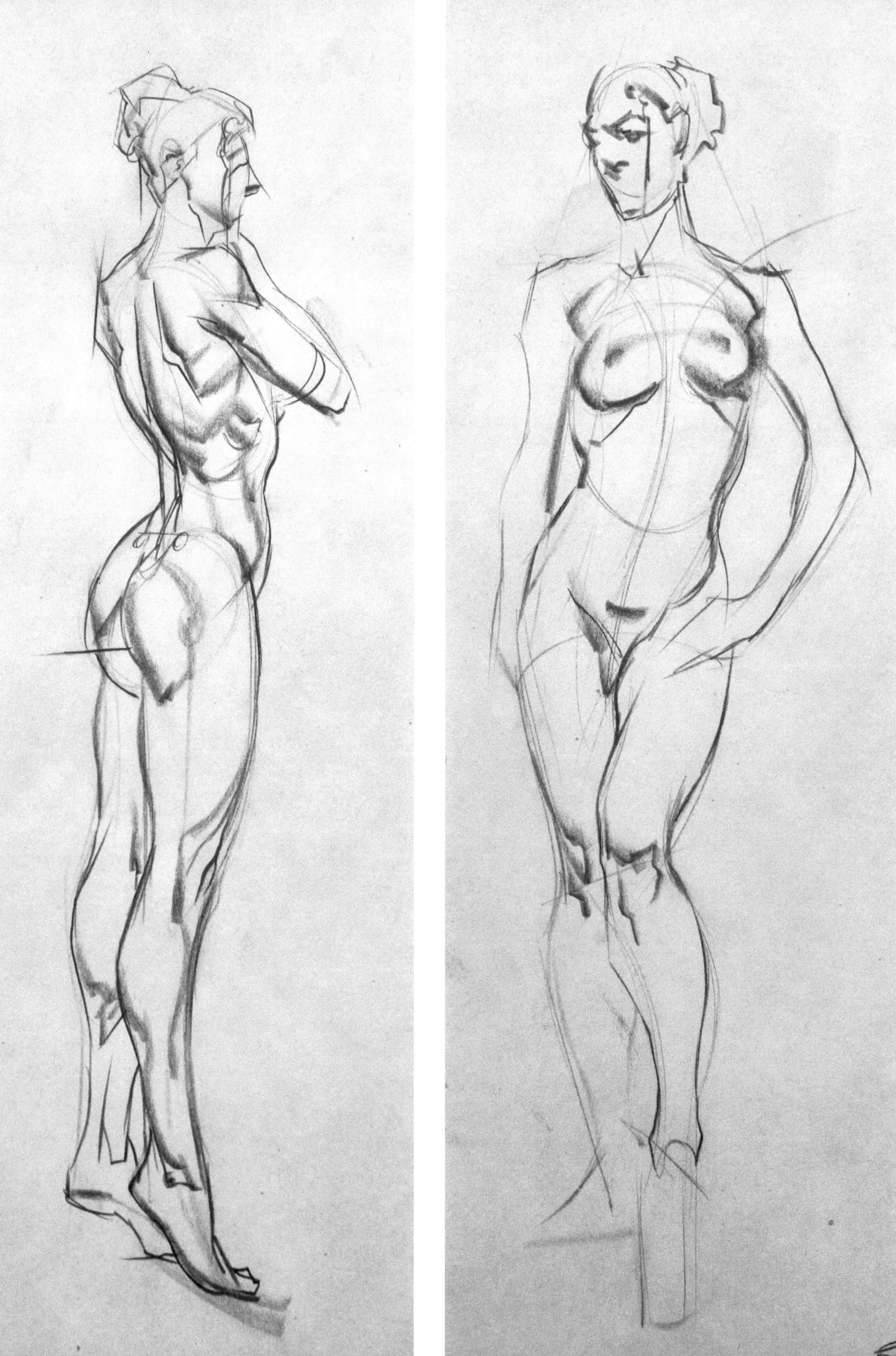

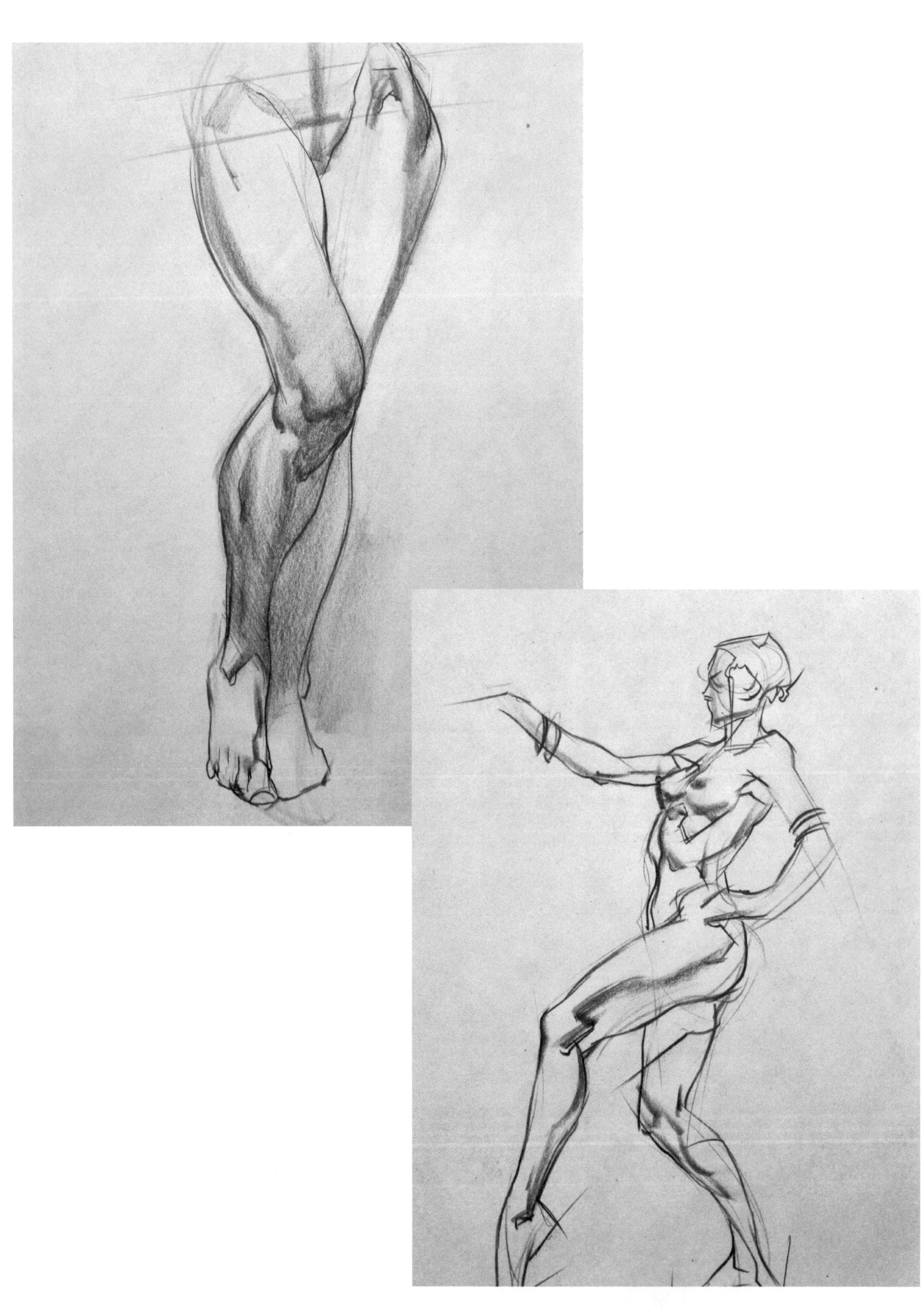

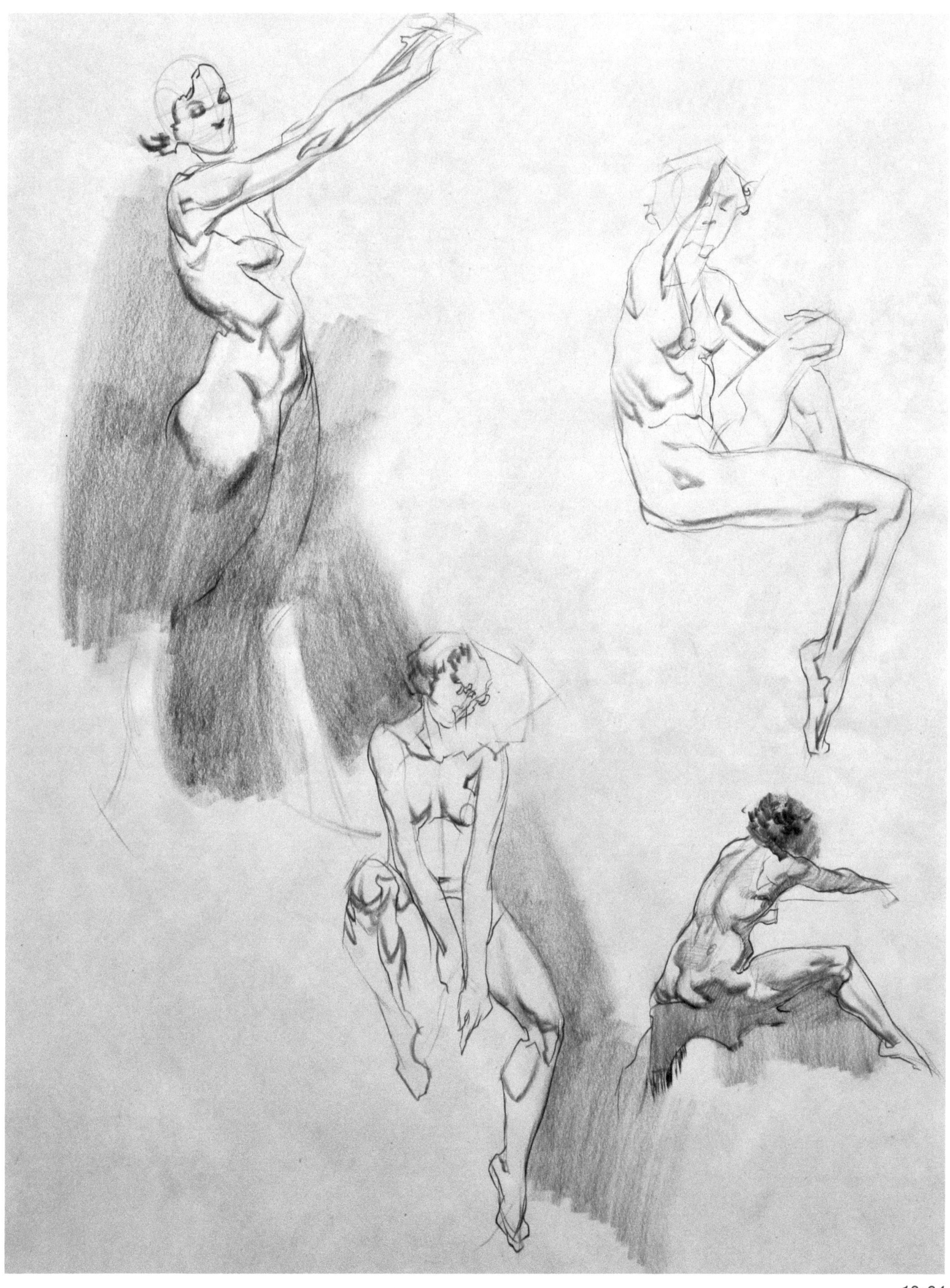

18x24
Charcoal/Newsprint
Quicksketch

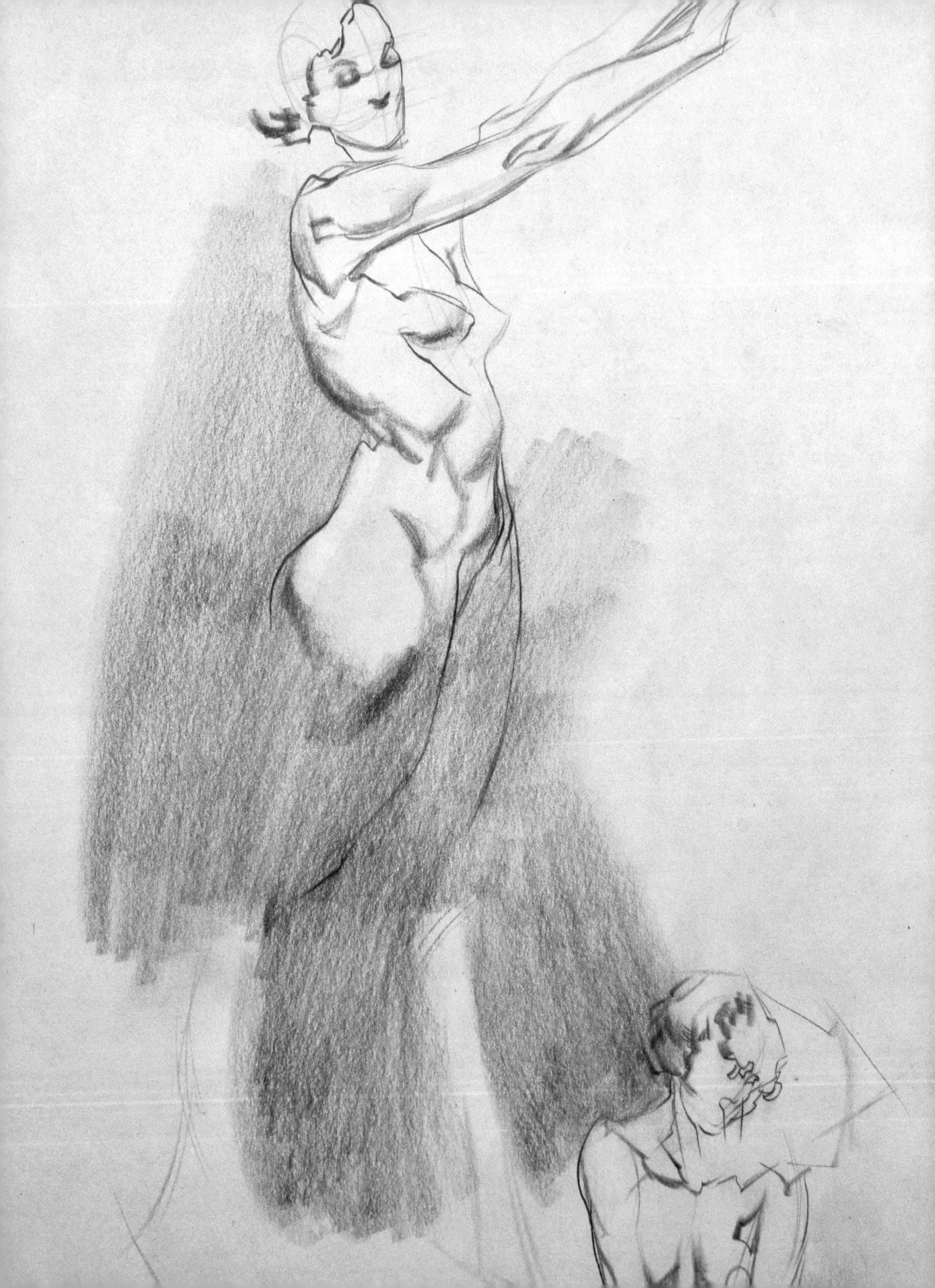

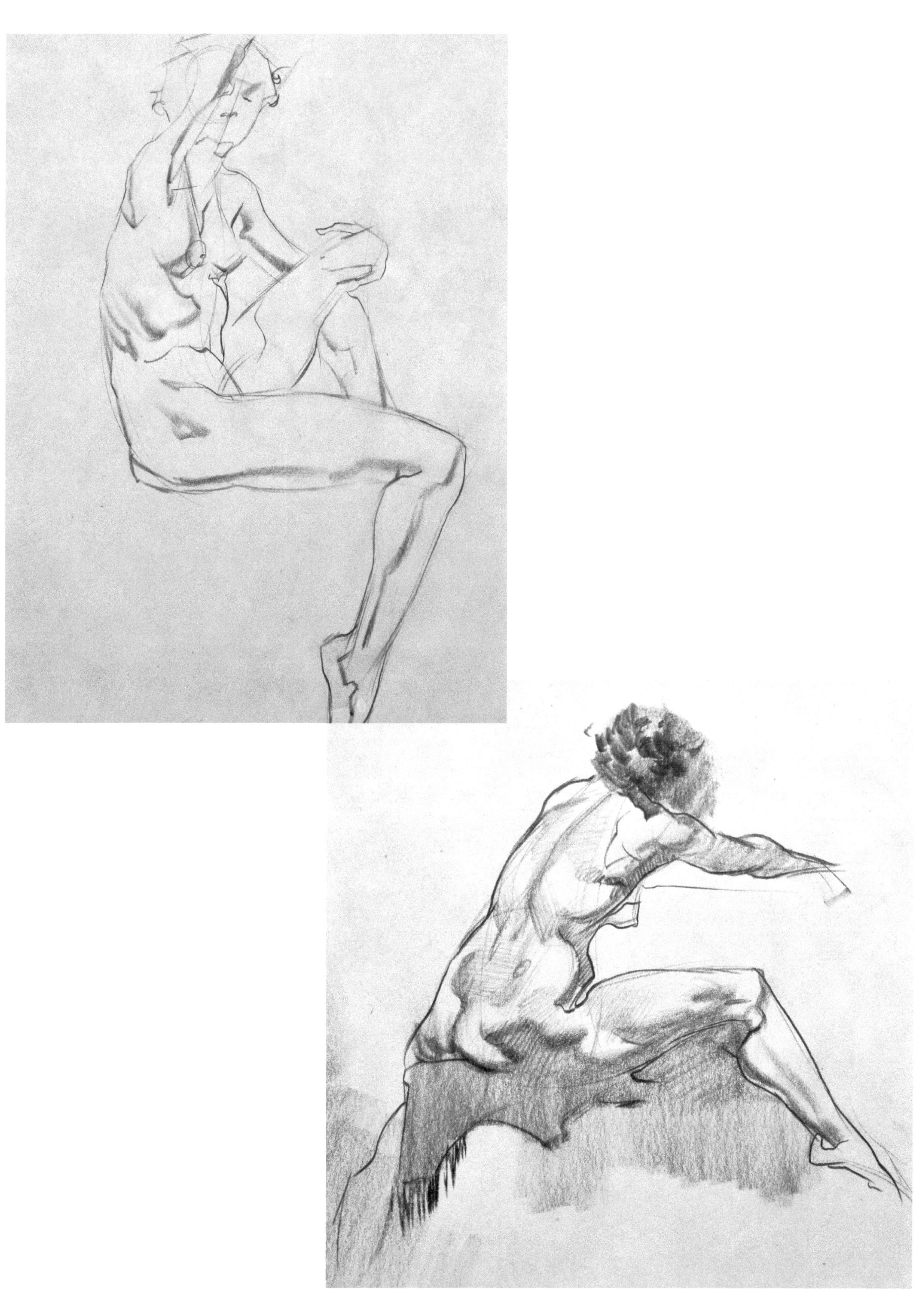

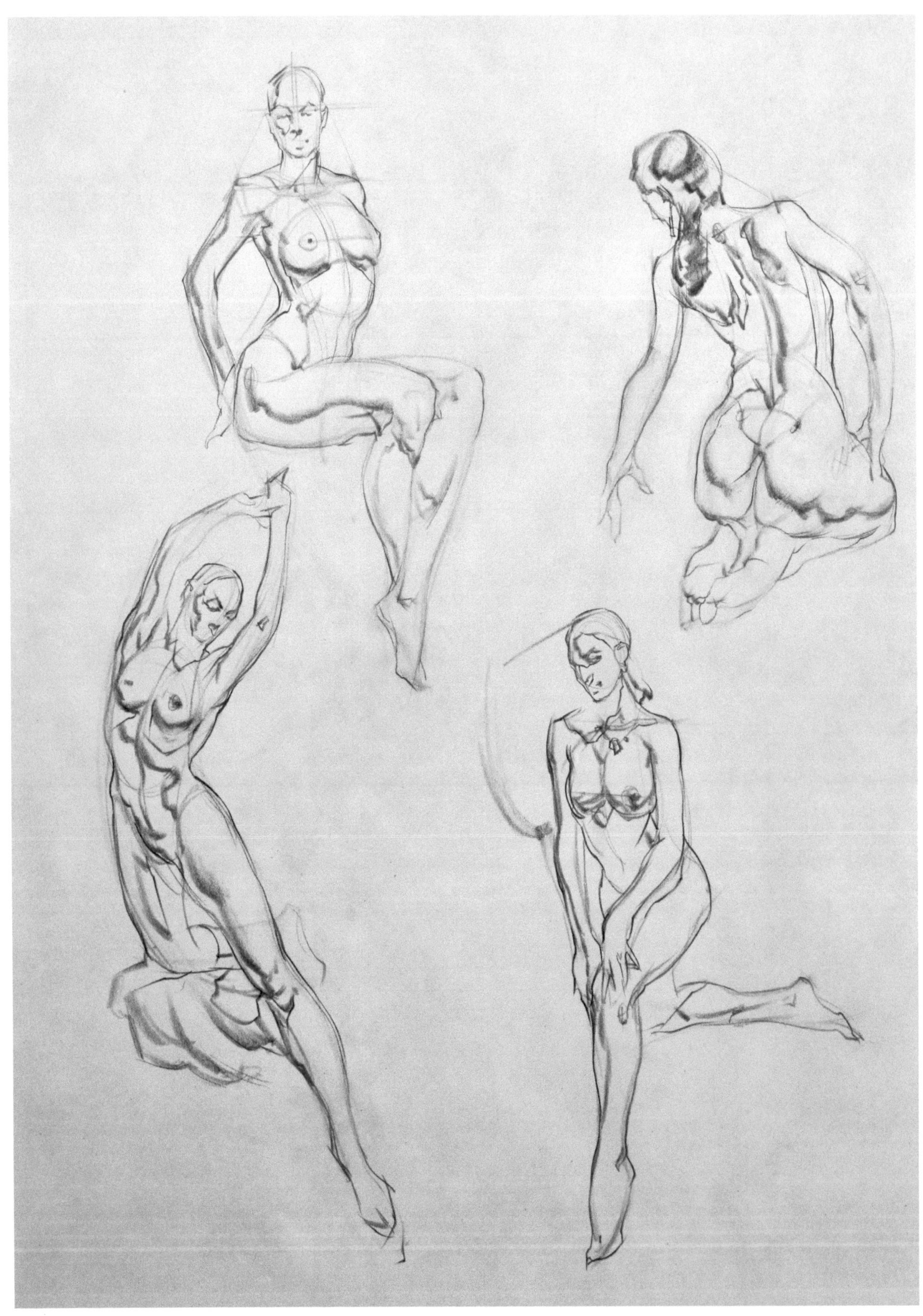

18x24
Charcoal/Newsprint
Quicksketch

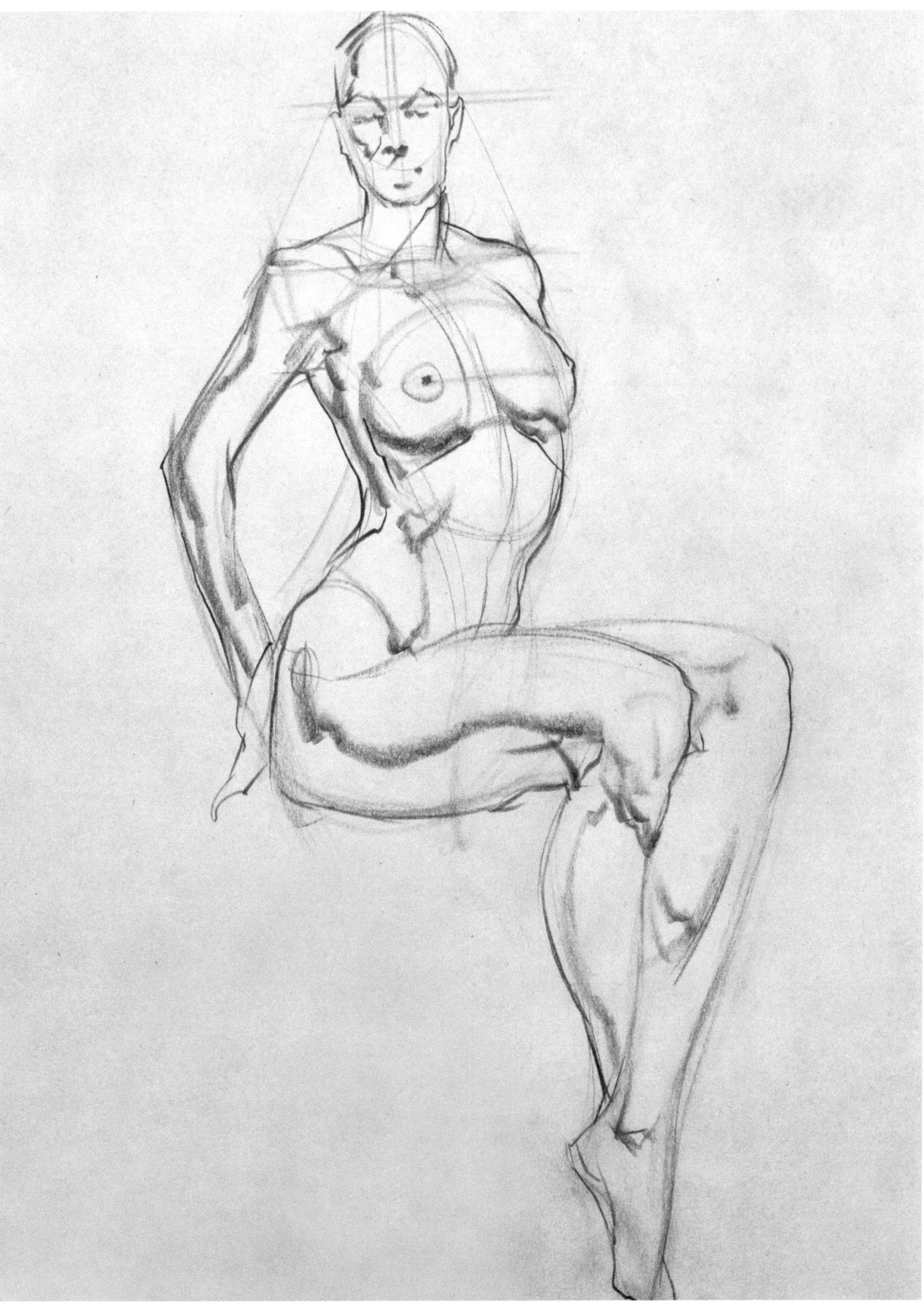

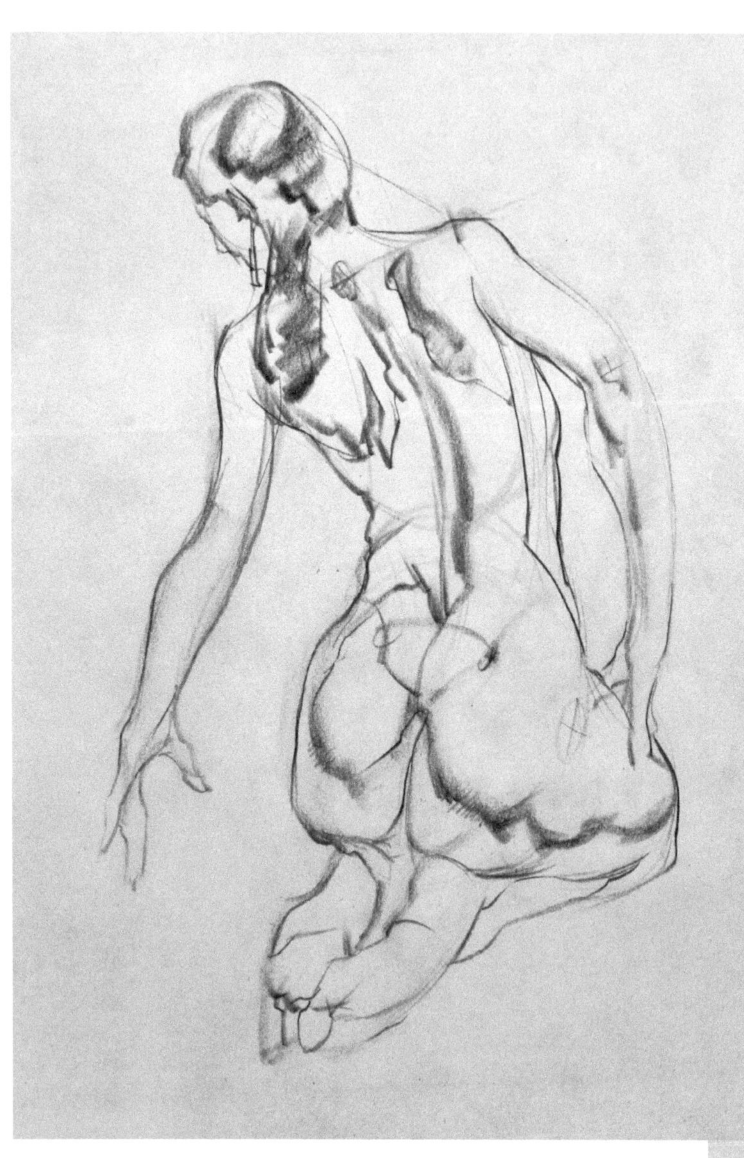

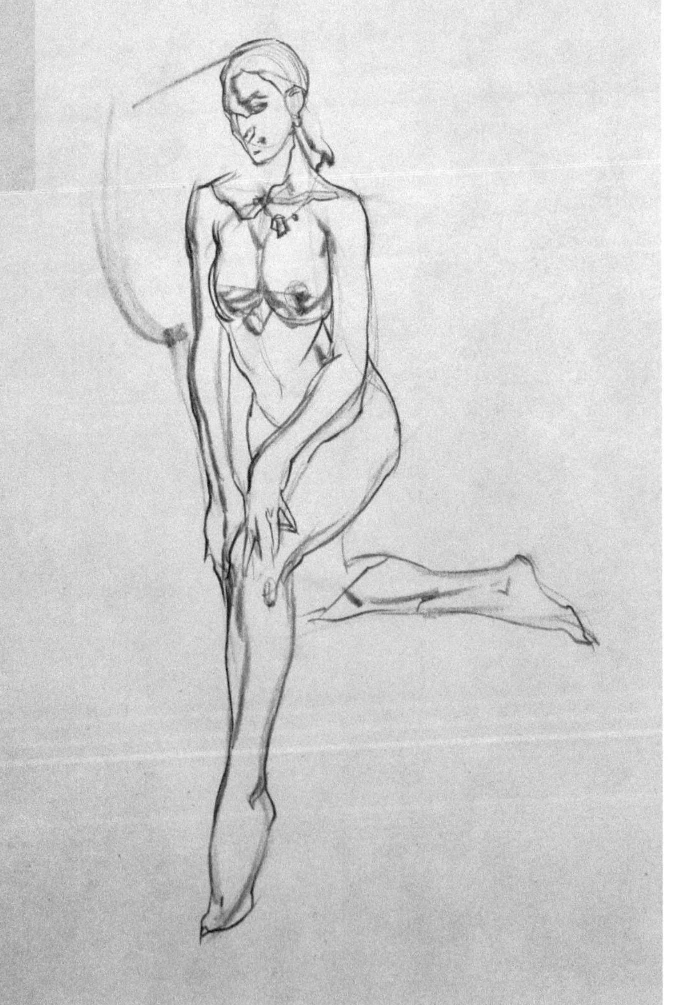

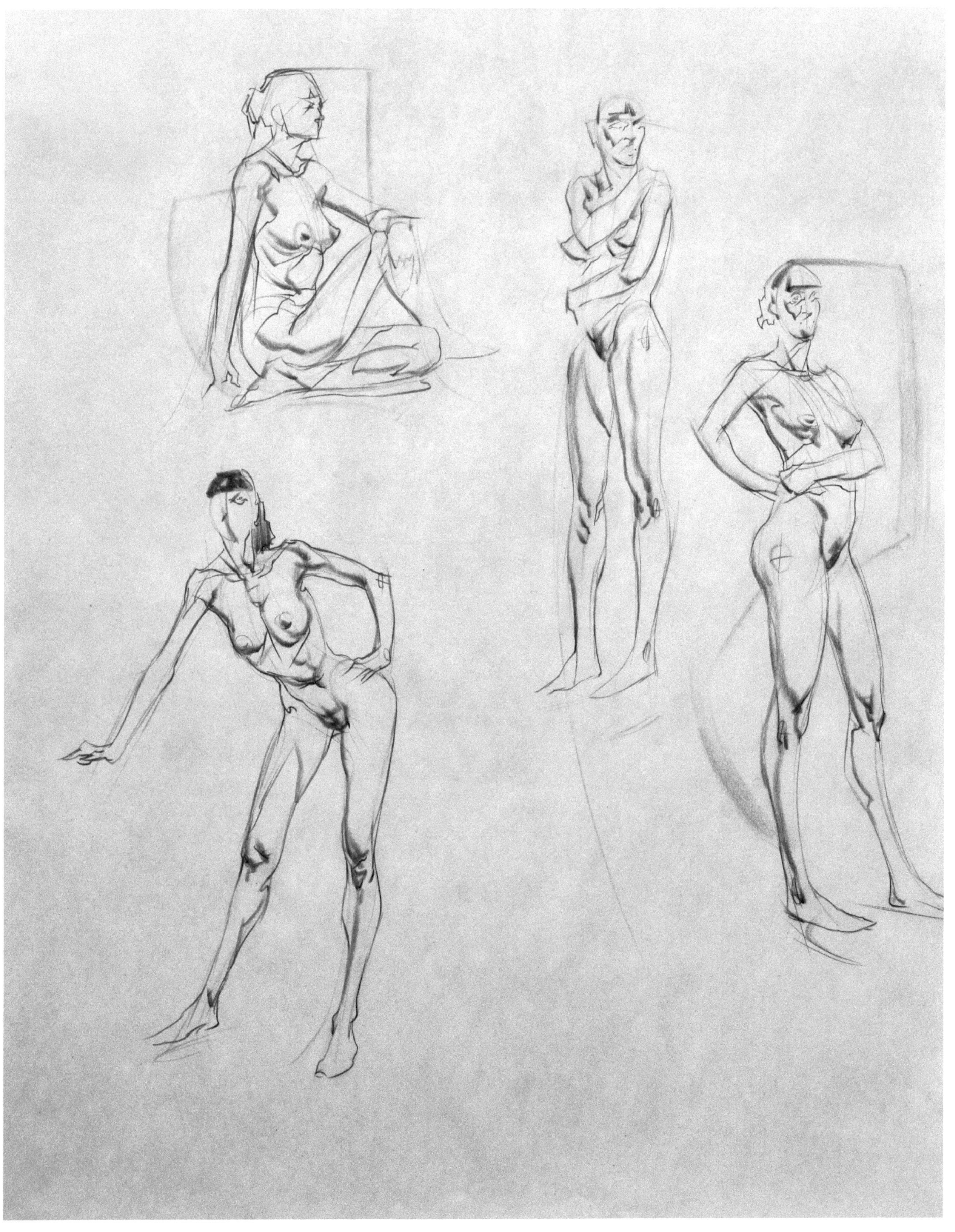

18x24
Charcoal/Newsprint
Quicksketch

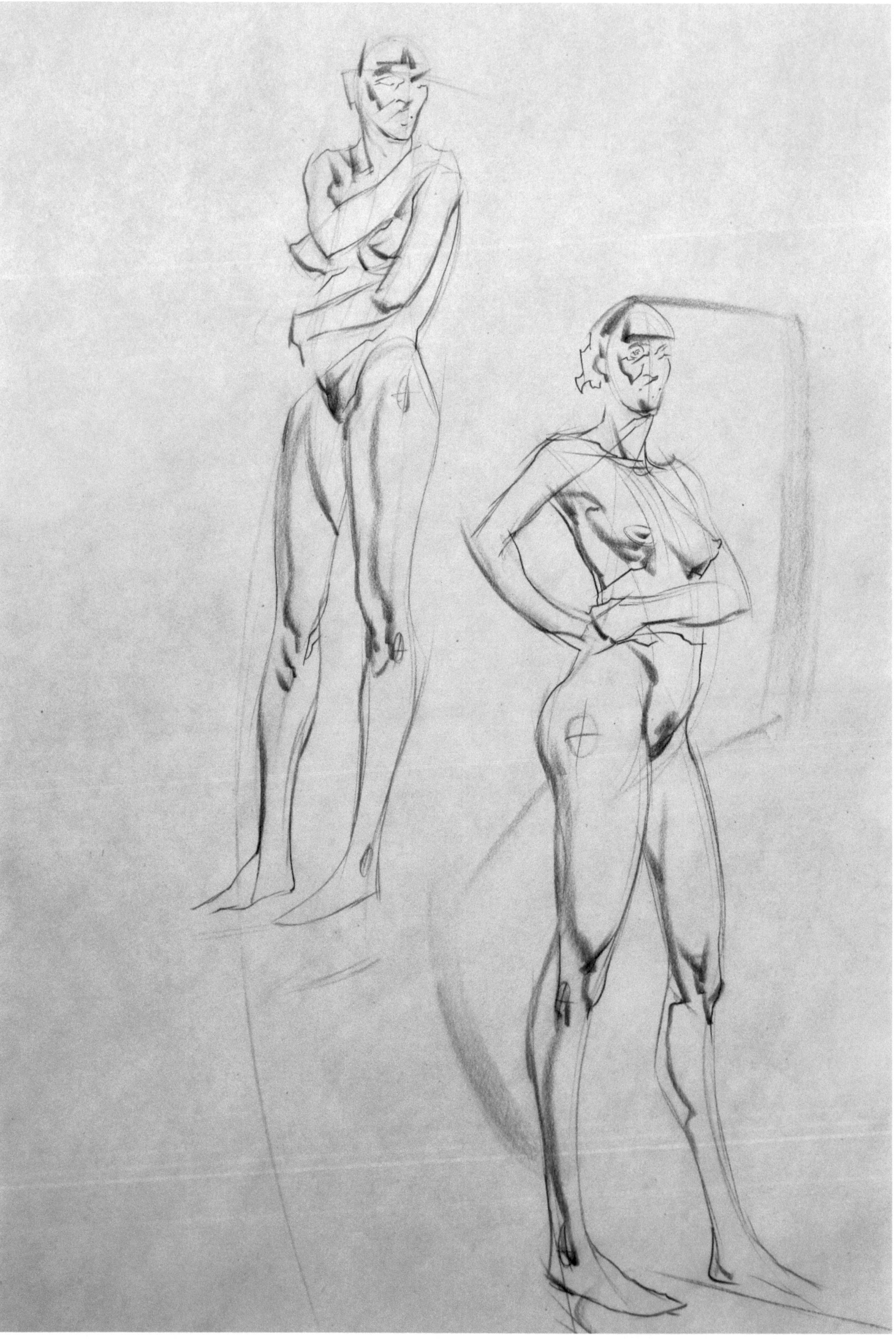

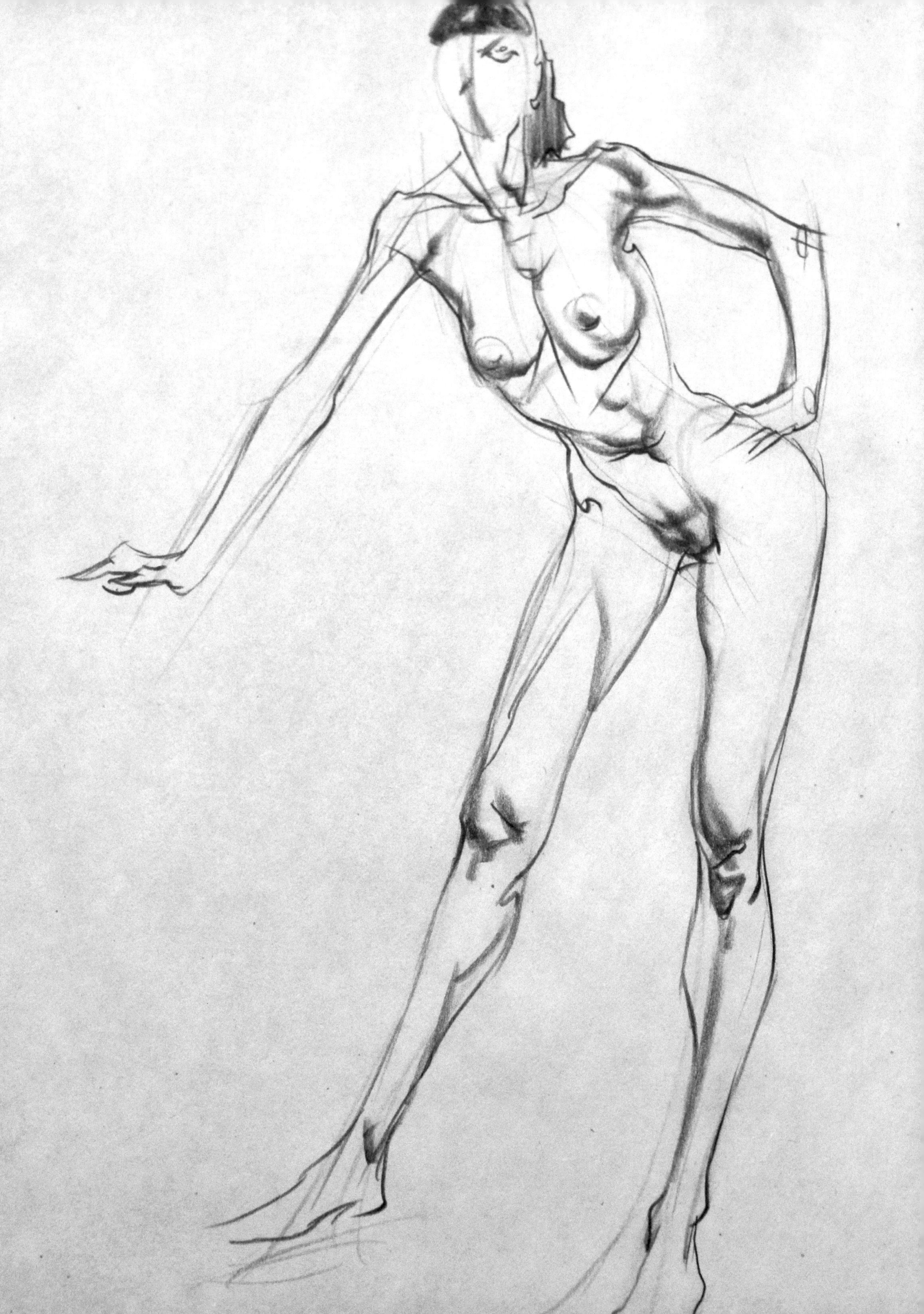

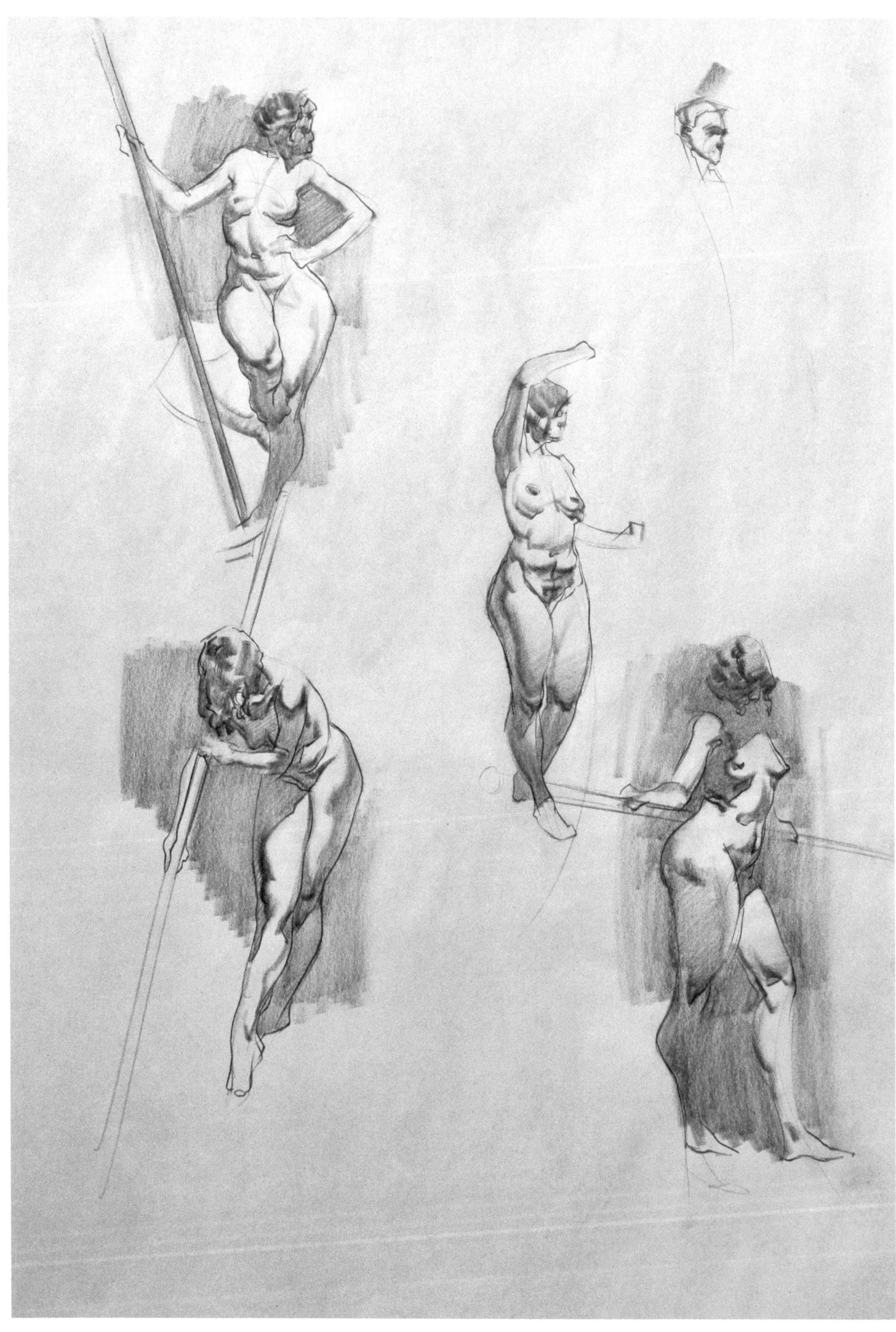

18x24
Charcoal/Newsprint
Quicksketch

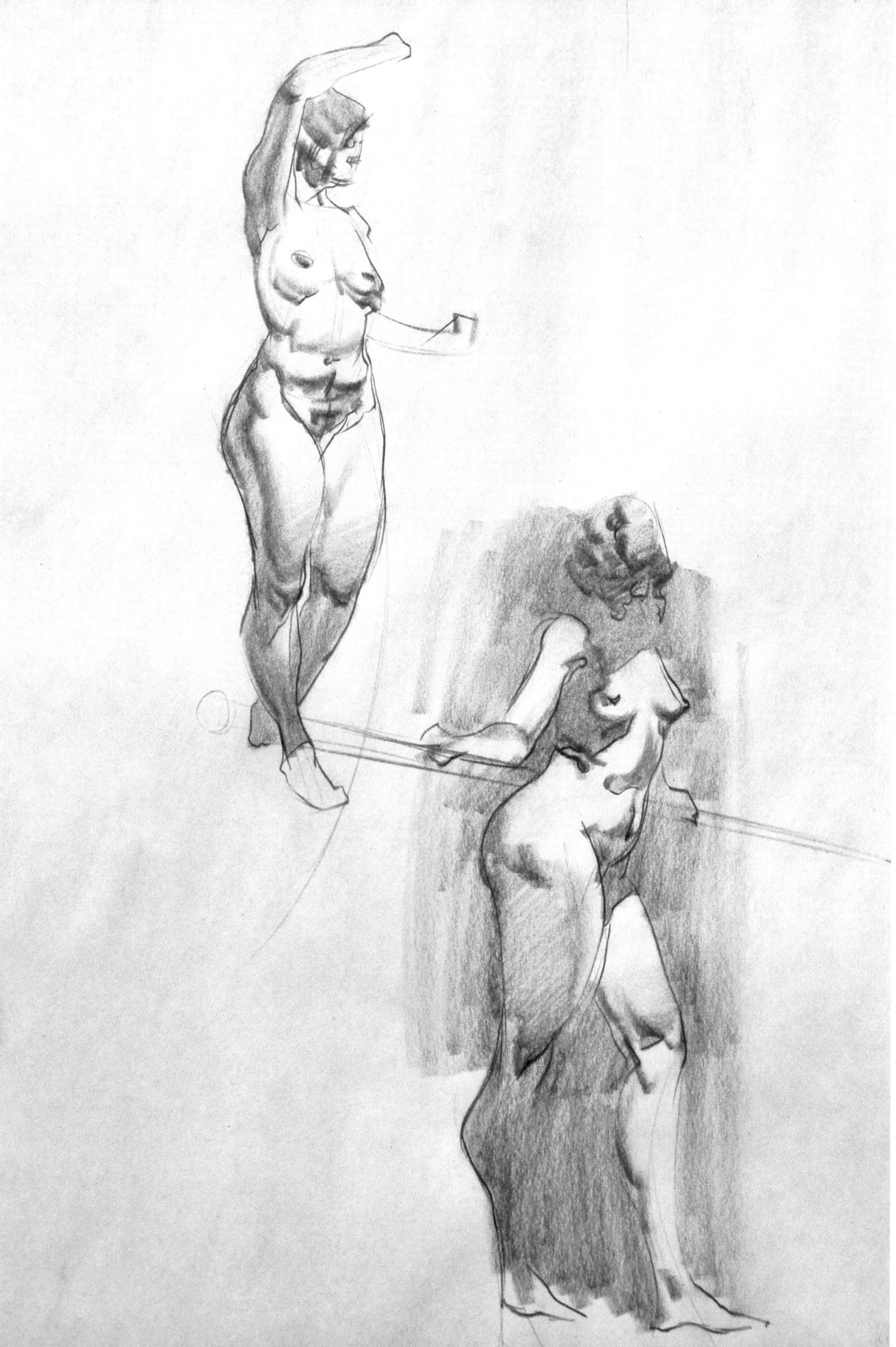

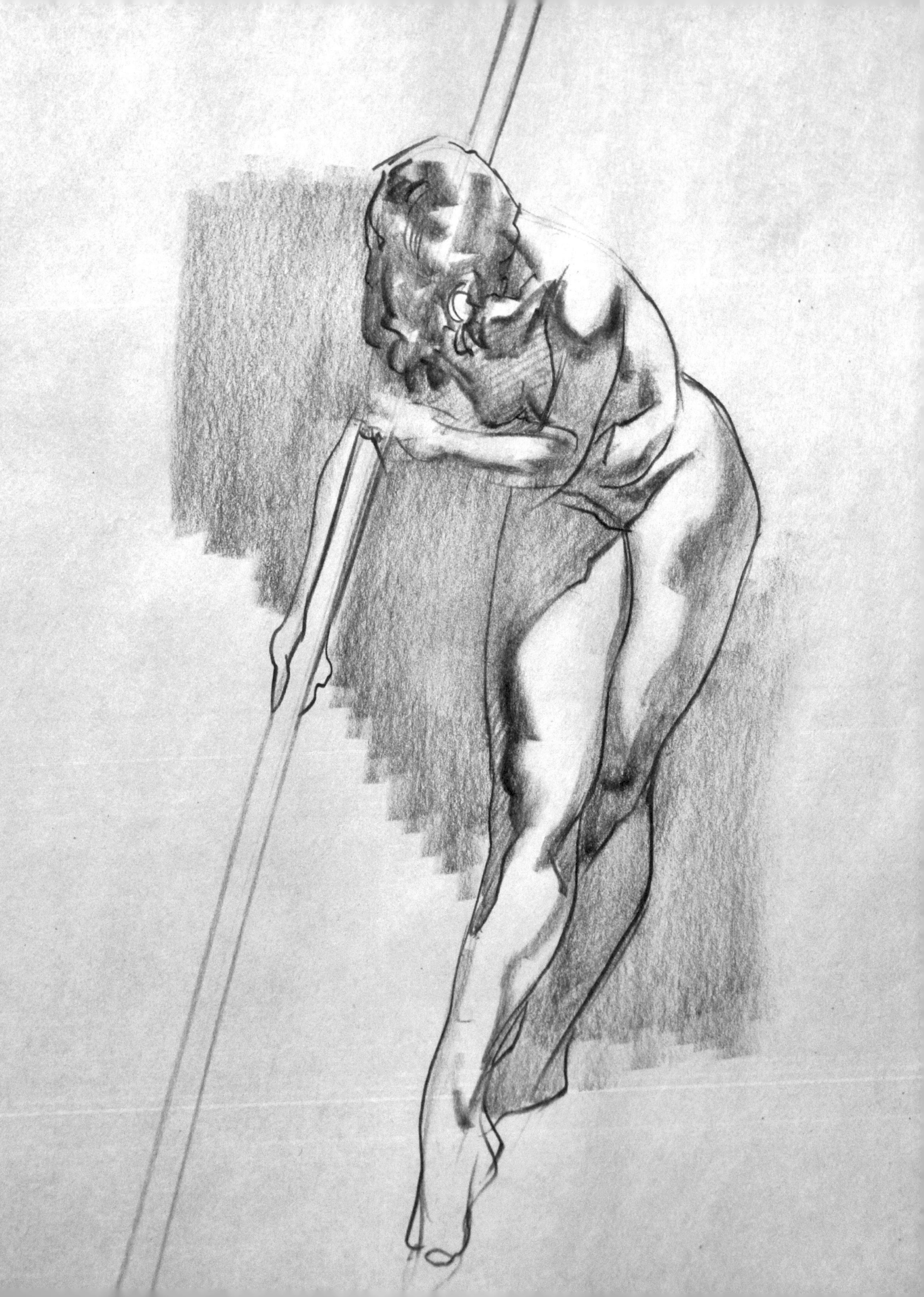

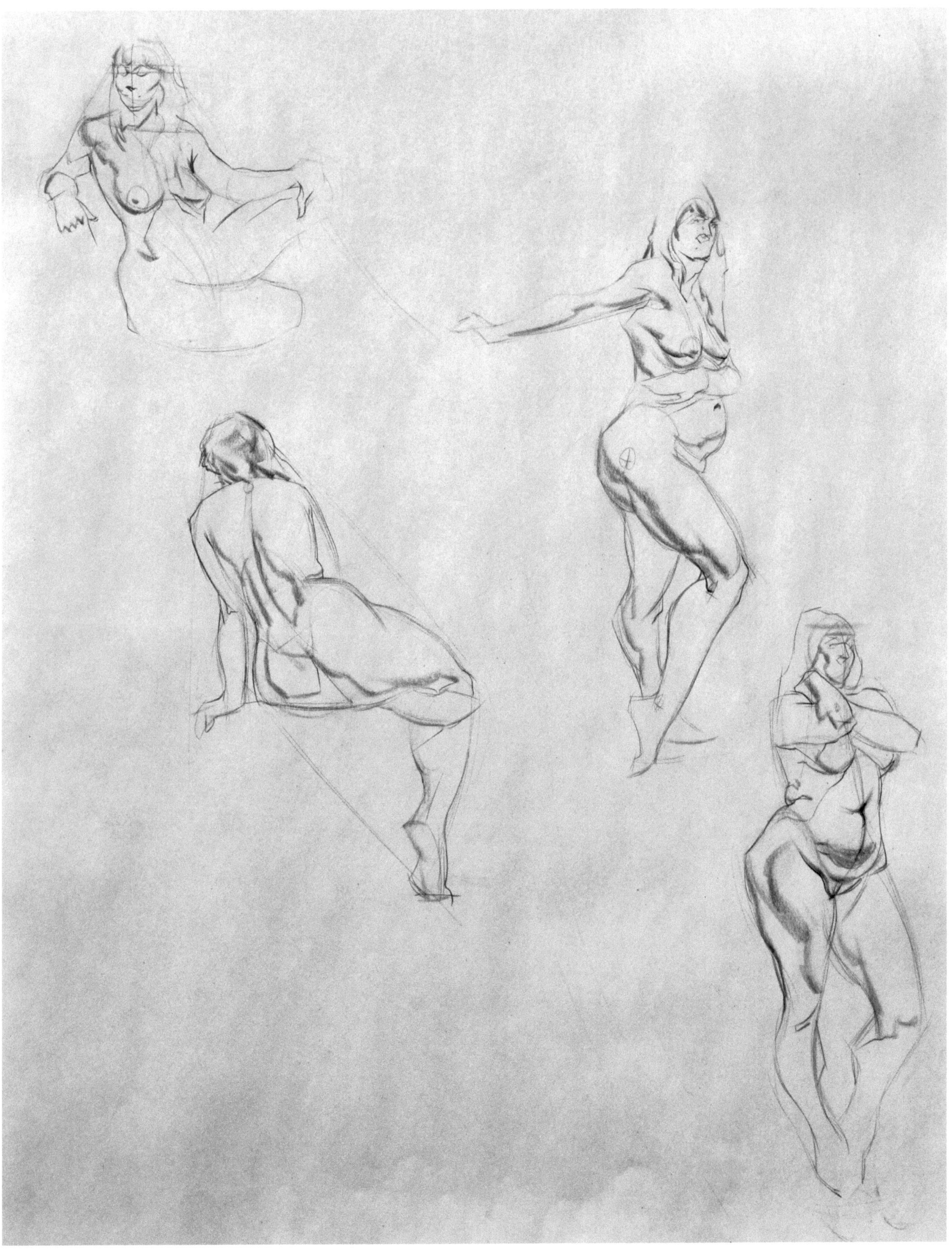

18x24
Charcoal/Newsprint
Quicksketch

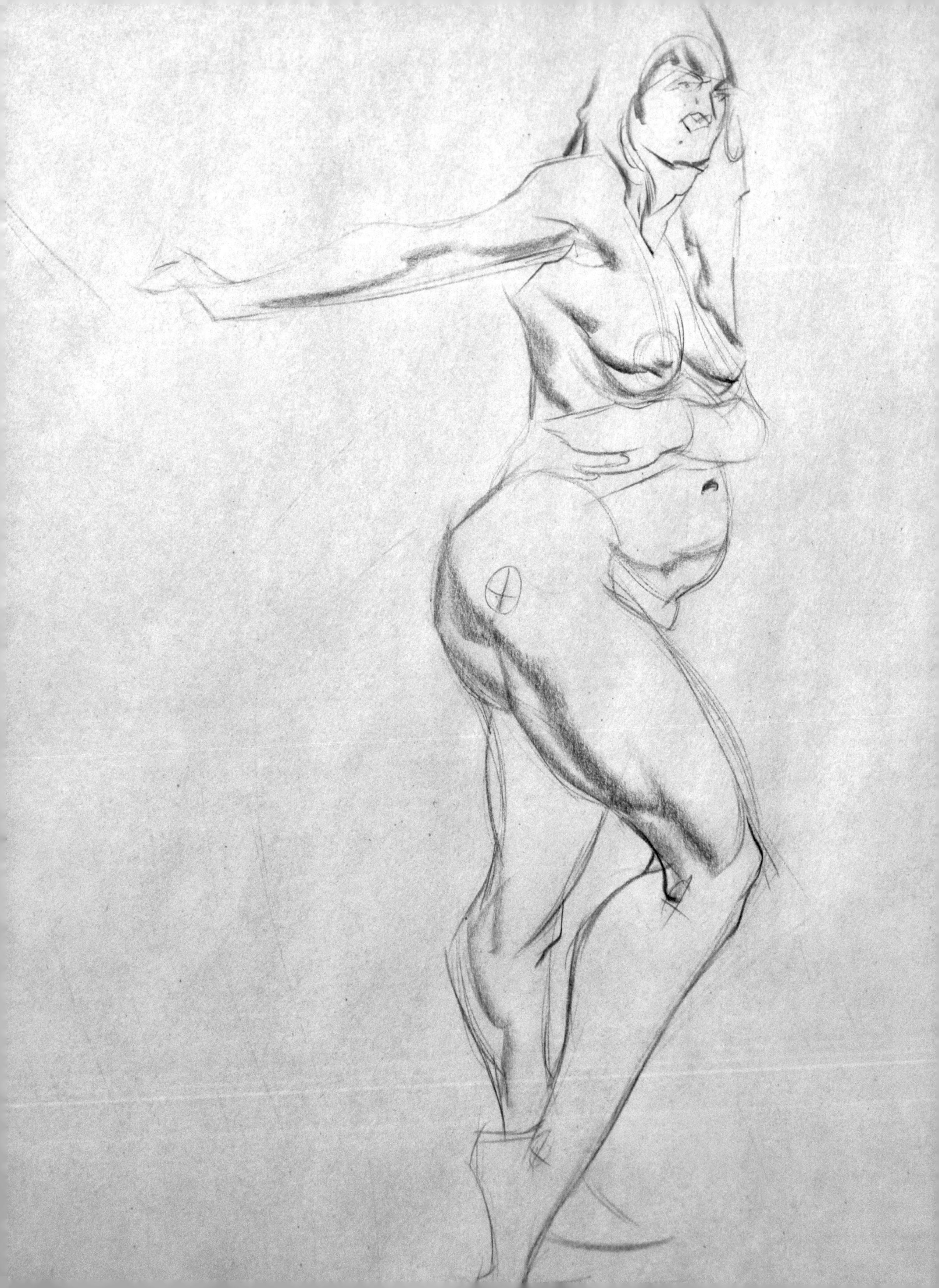

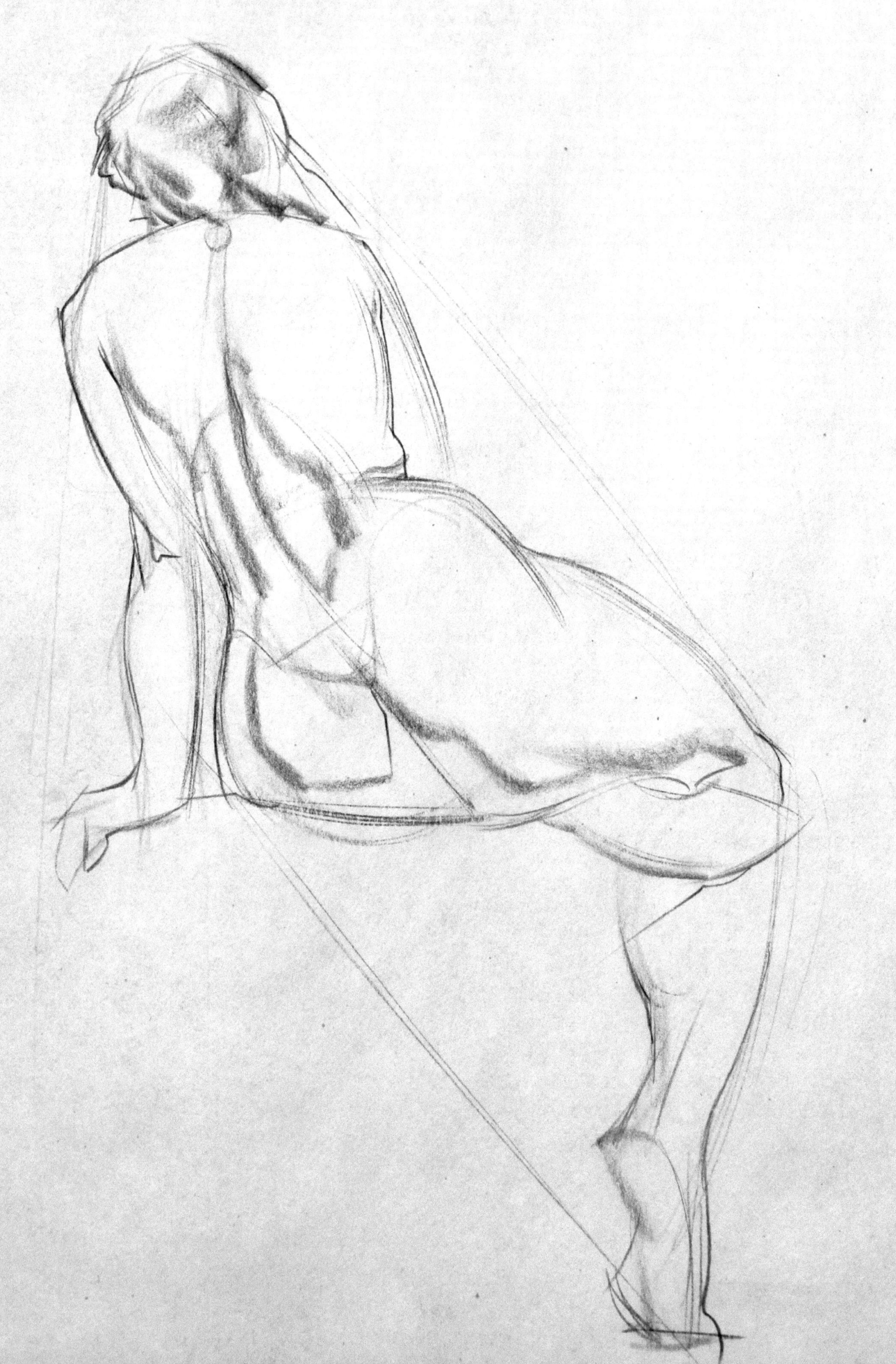

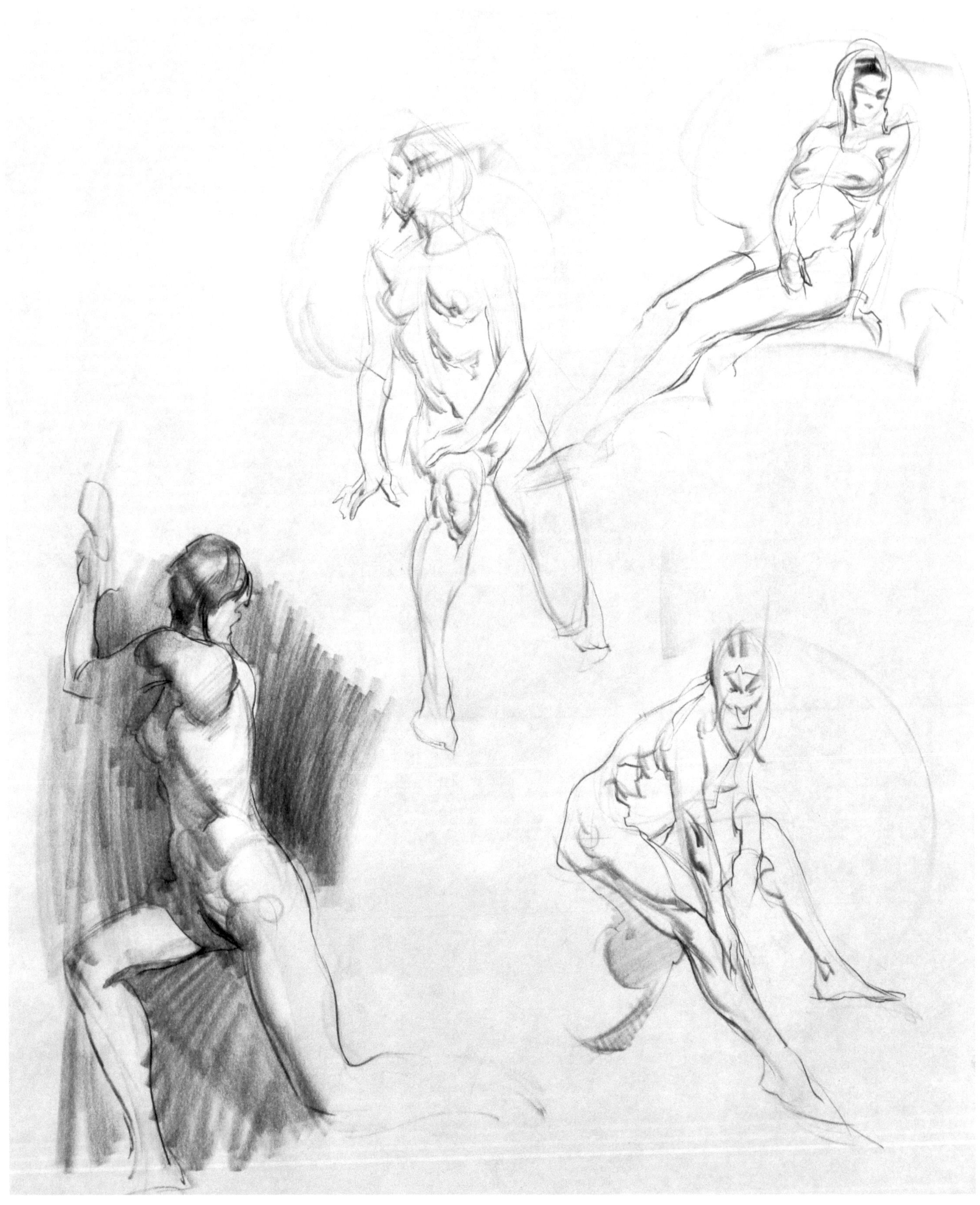

18x24
Charcoal/Newsprint
Quicksketch

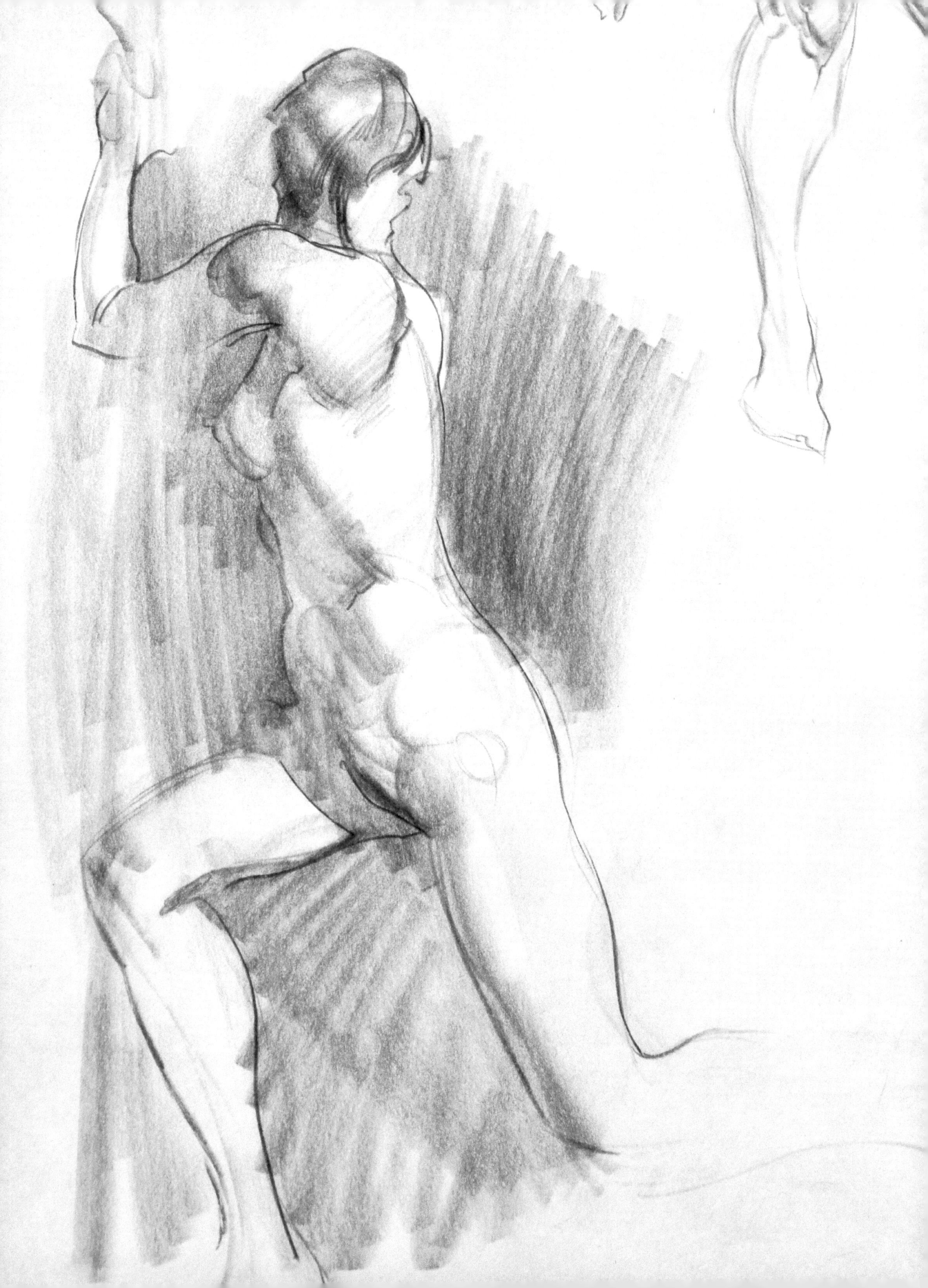

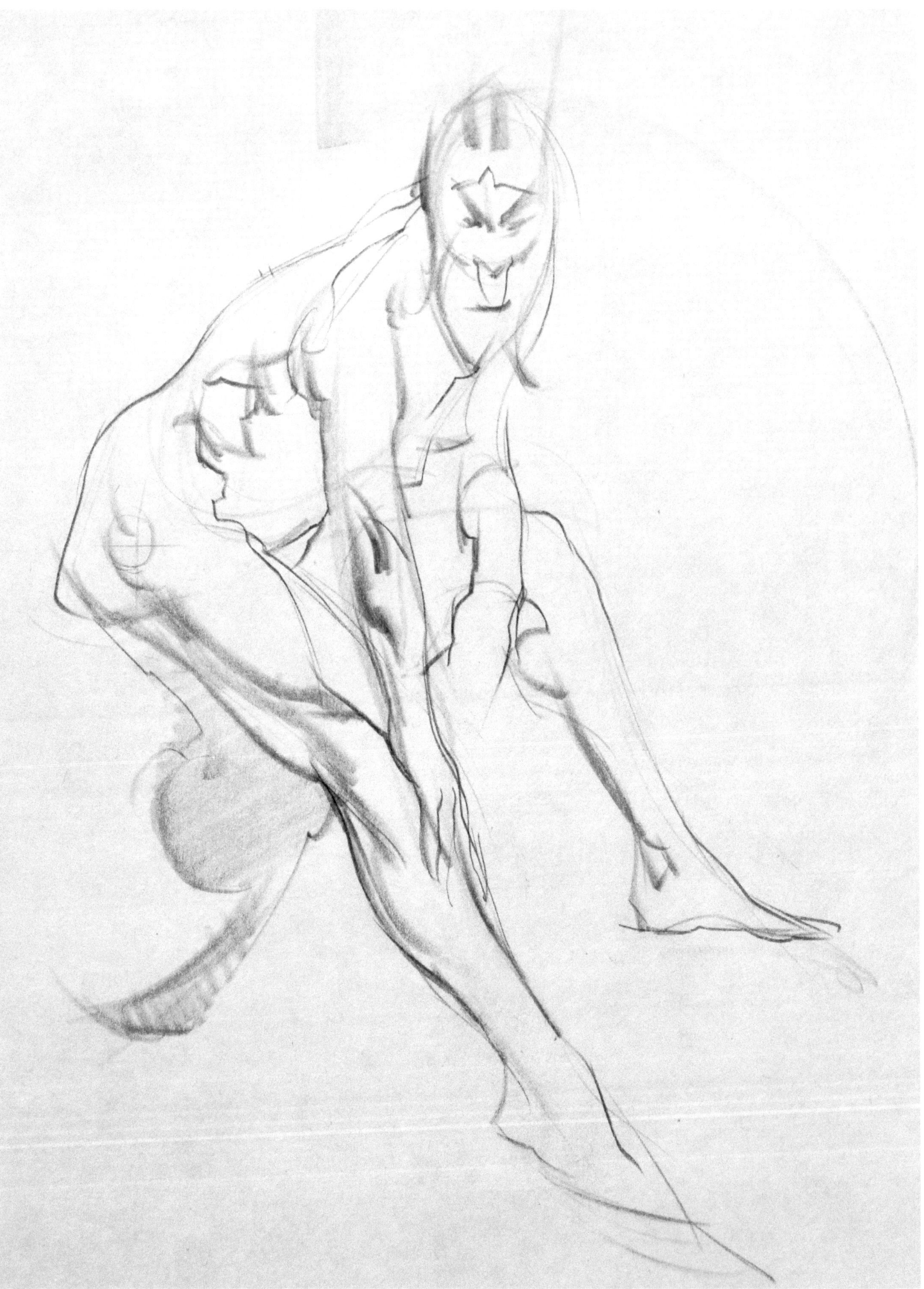

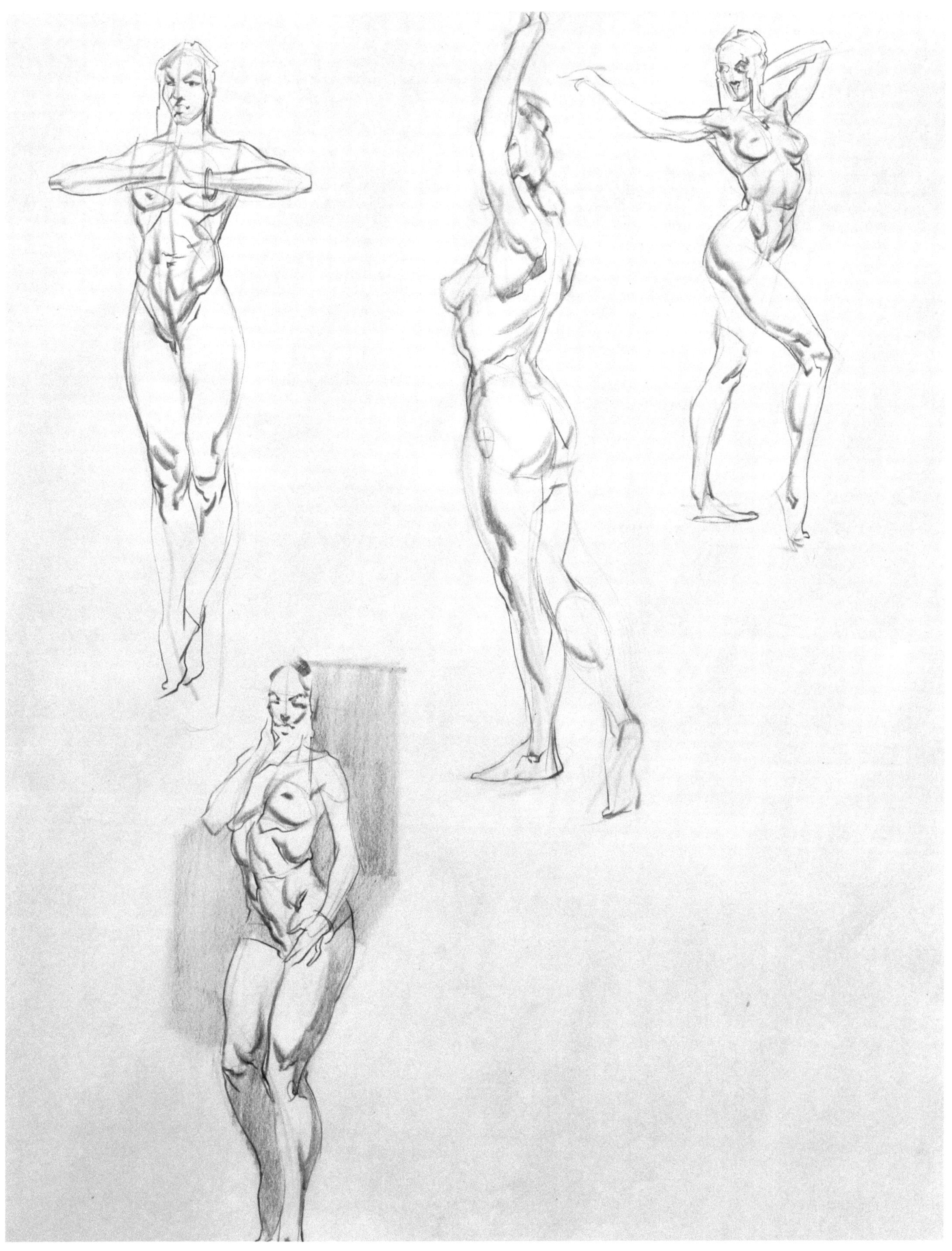

18x24
Charcoal/Newsprint
Quicksketch

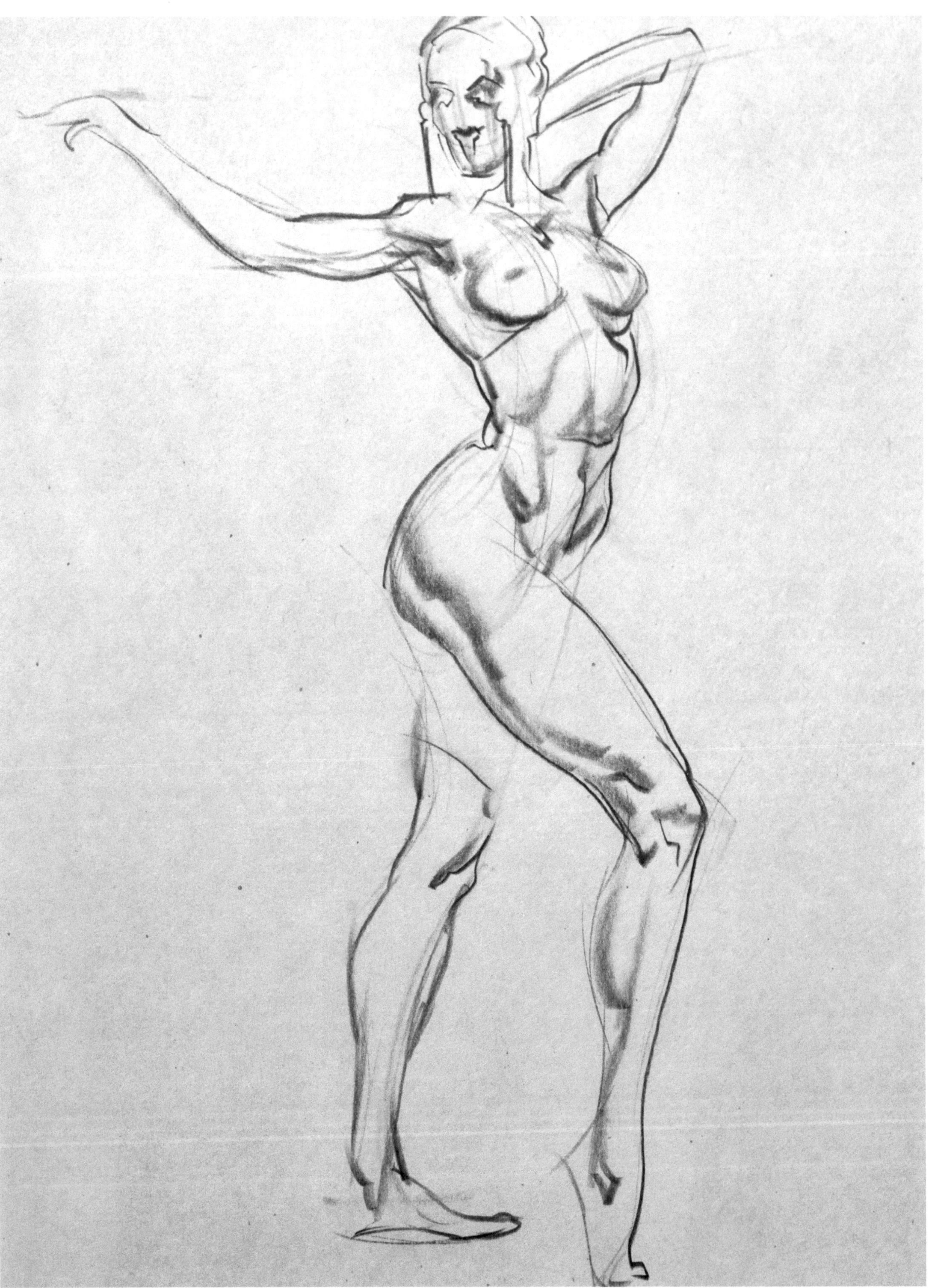

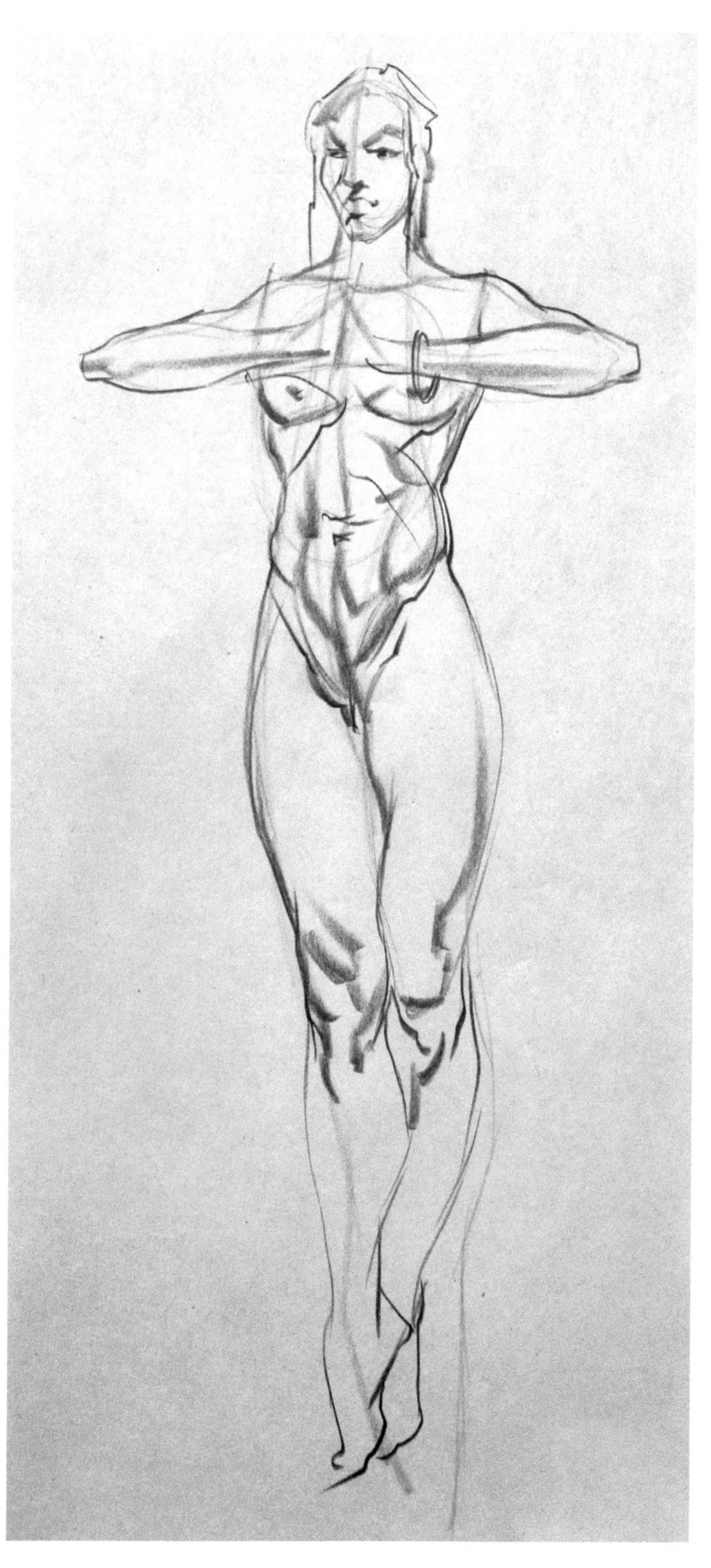
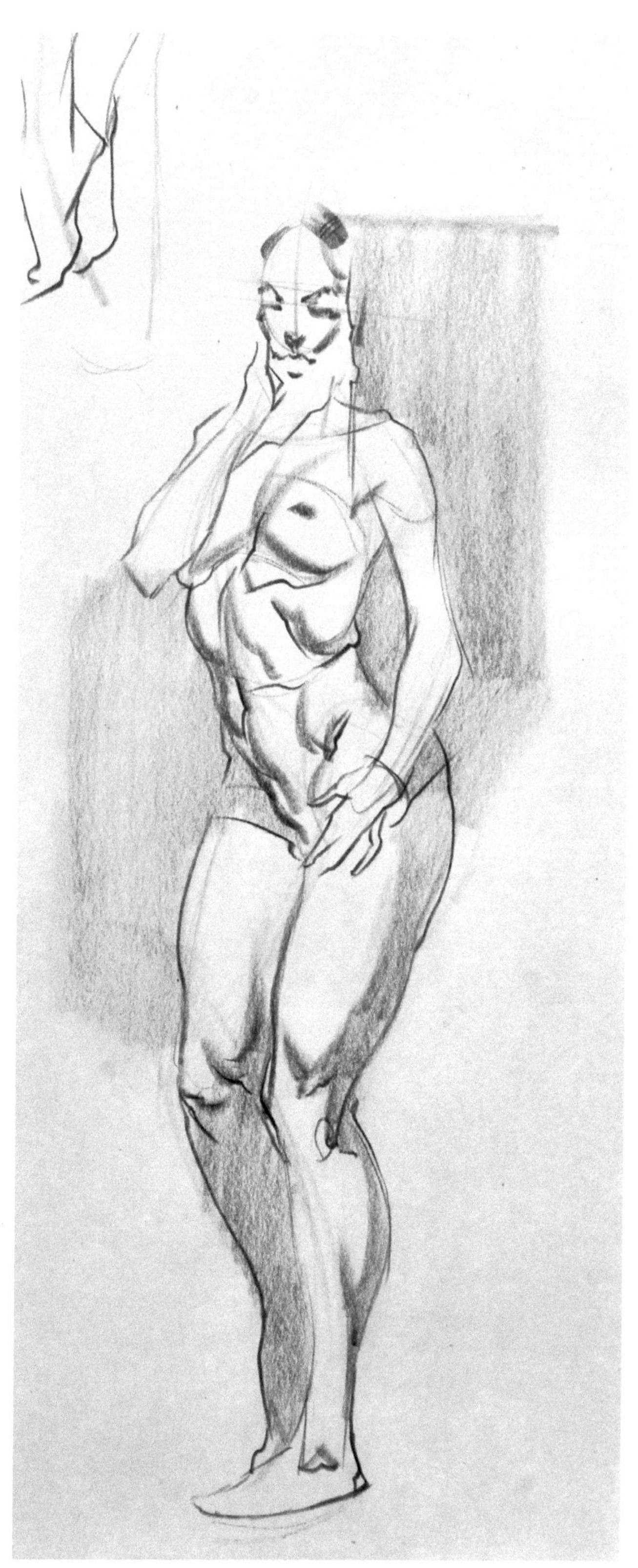

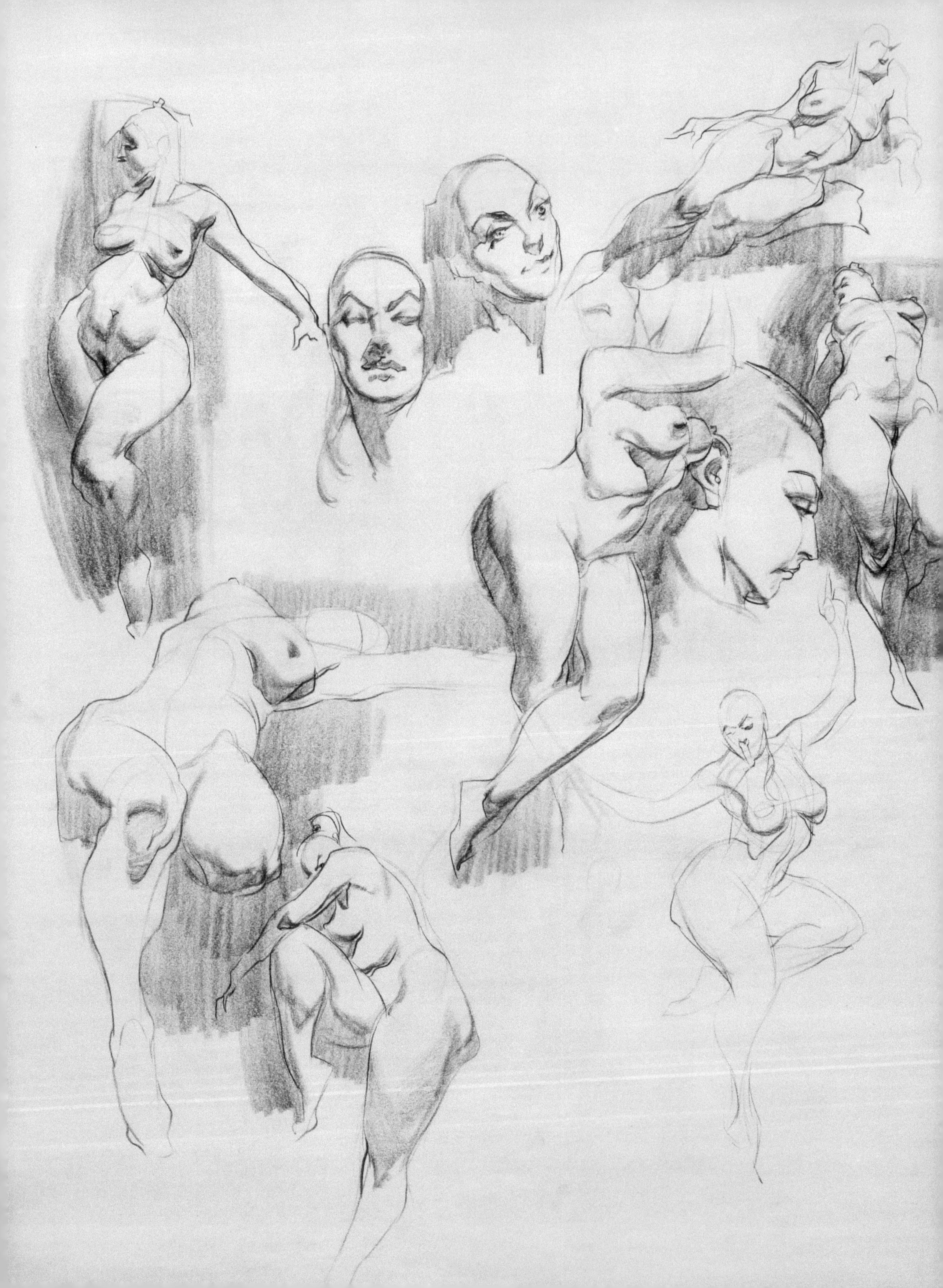

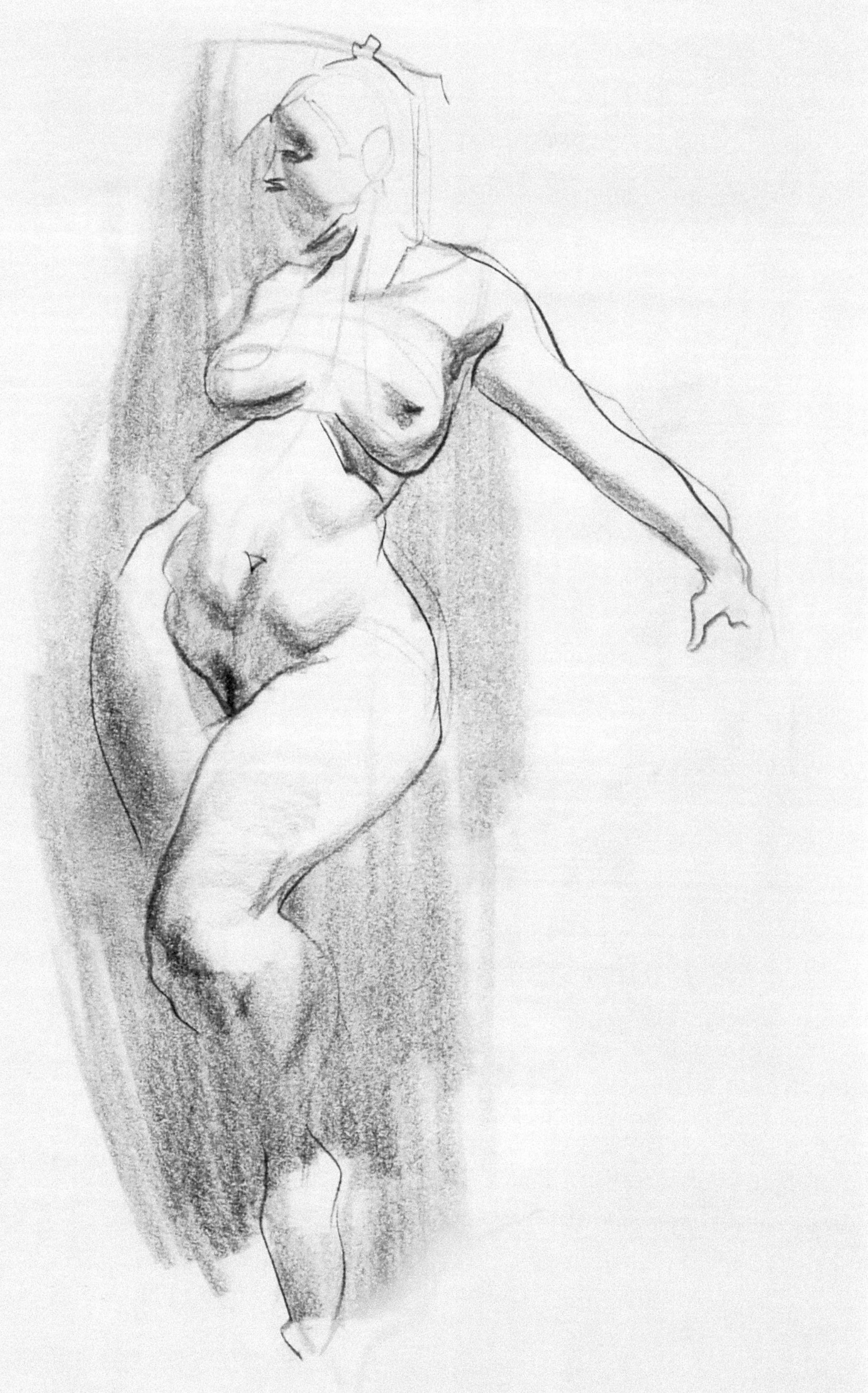

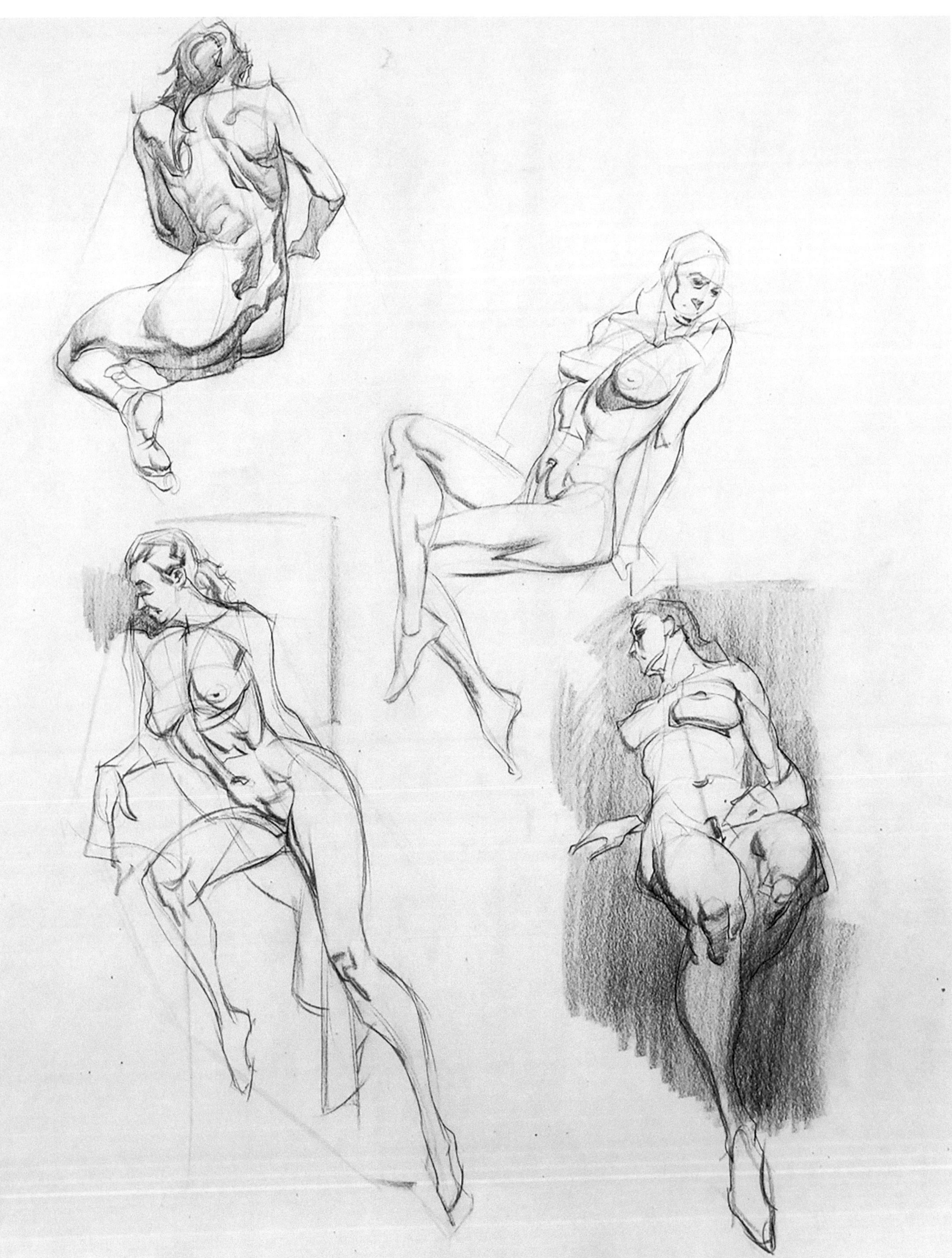

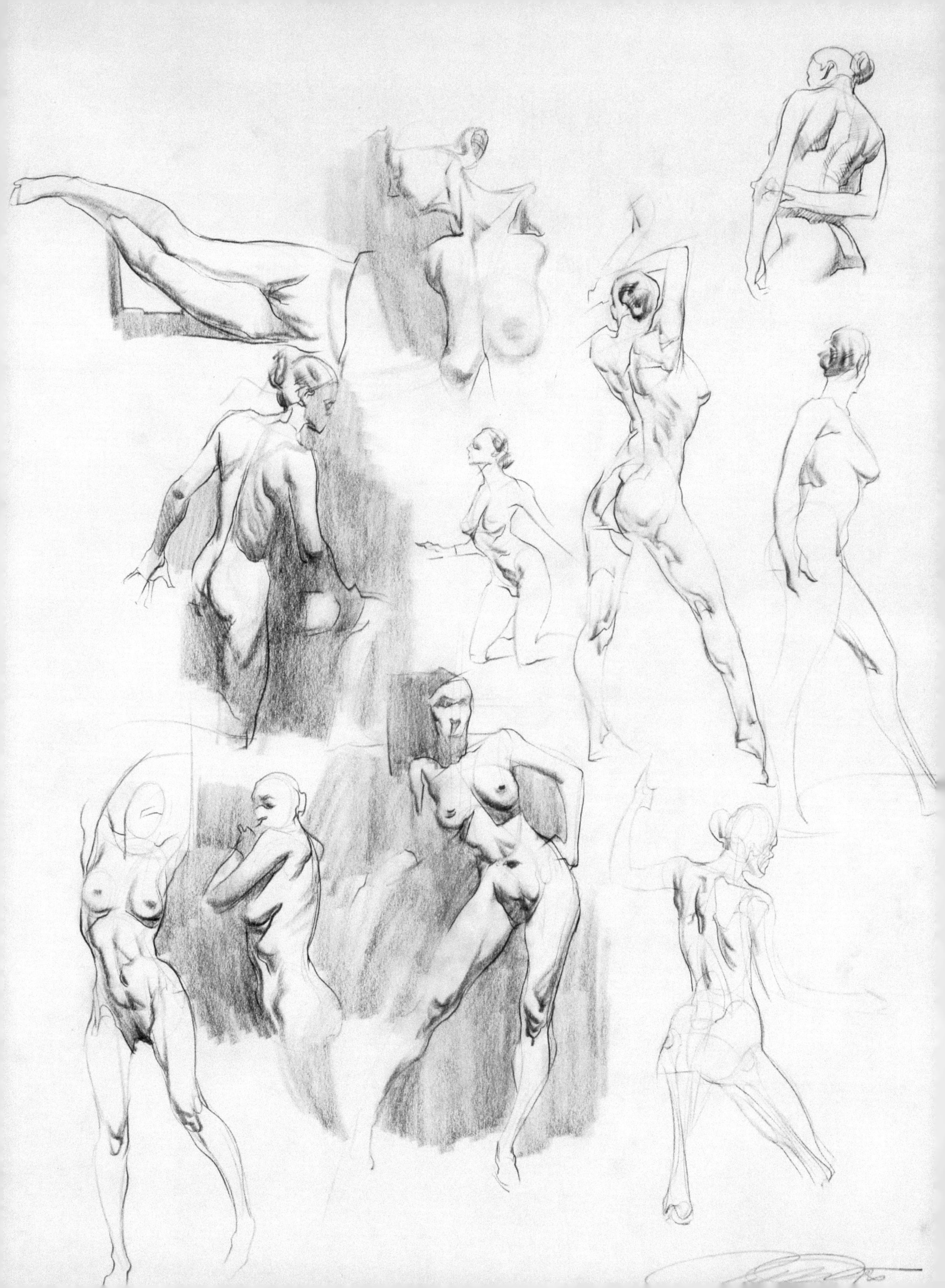

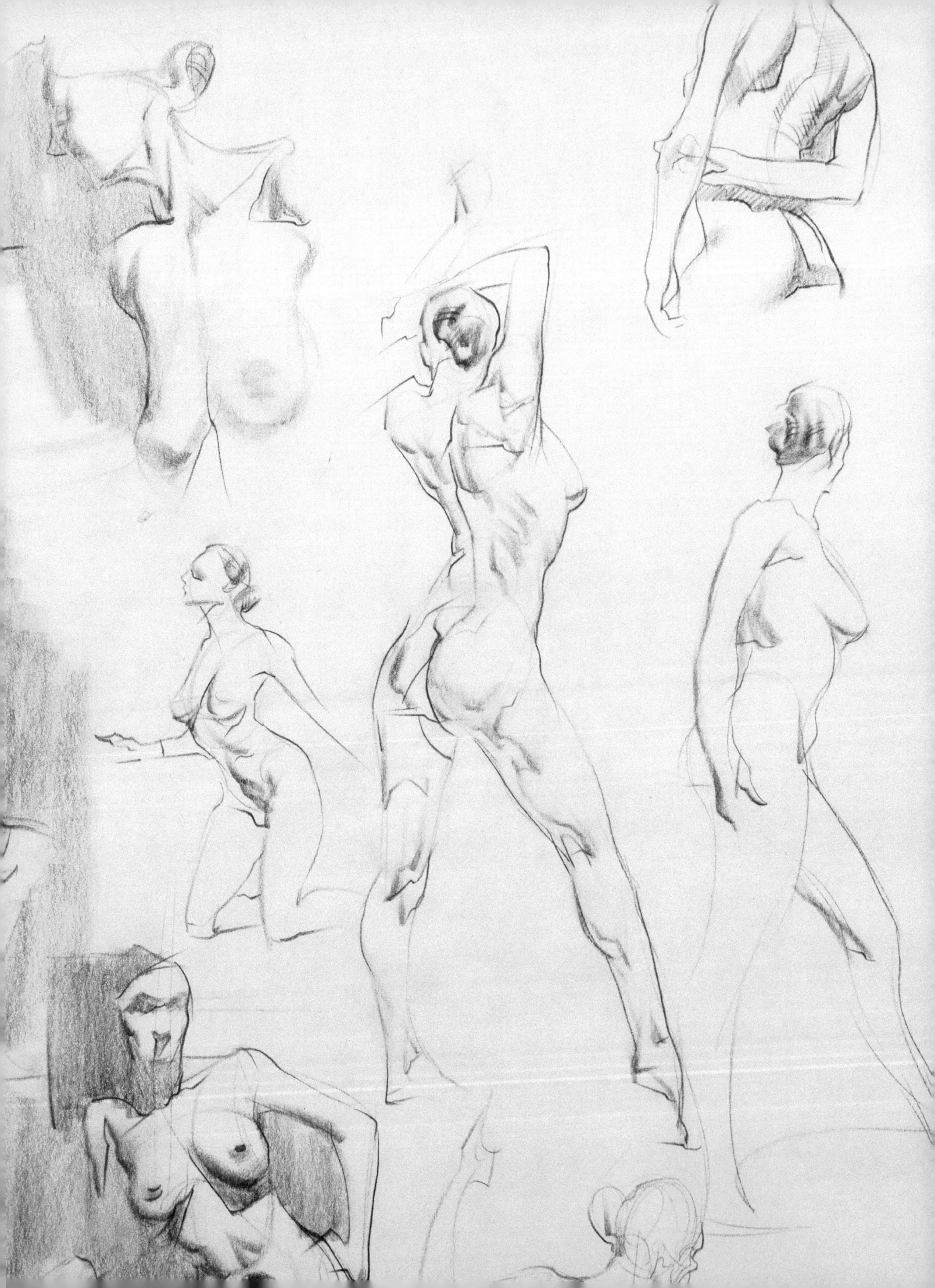

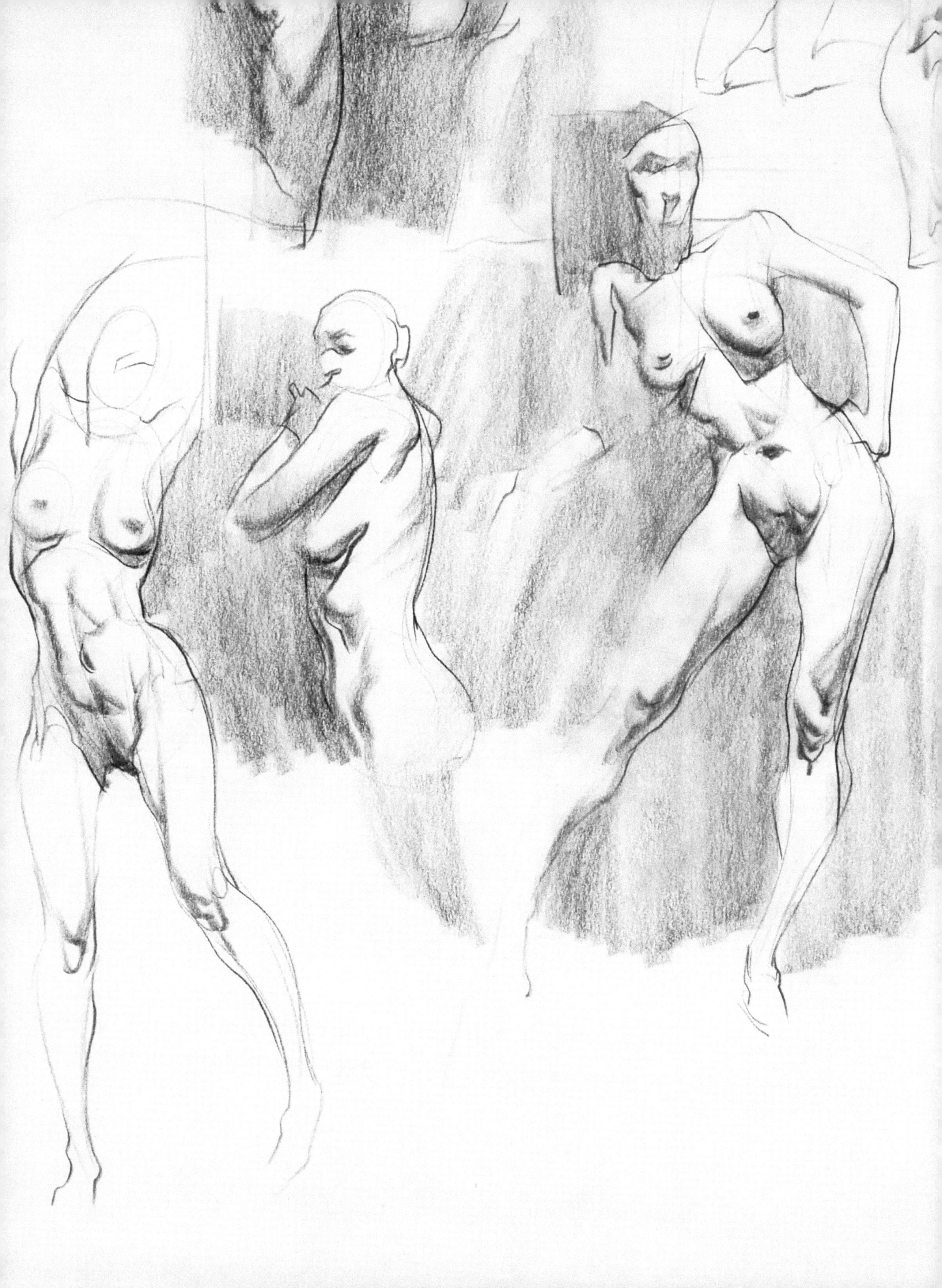

WATTS ATELIER
— OF THE ARTS — LLC

ART — EDUCATION — VISION

WATTS ATELIER ONLINE PROGRAM
1000+ HOURS OF CONTENT
DRAWING • PAINTING • DESIGN
START YOUR JOURNEY TODAY, ENROLL AT
www.WATTSATELIER.com

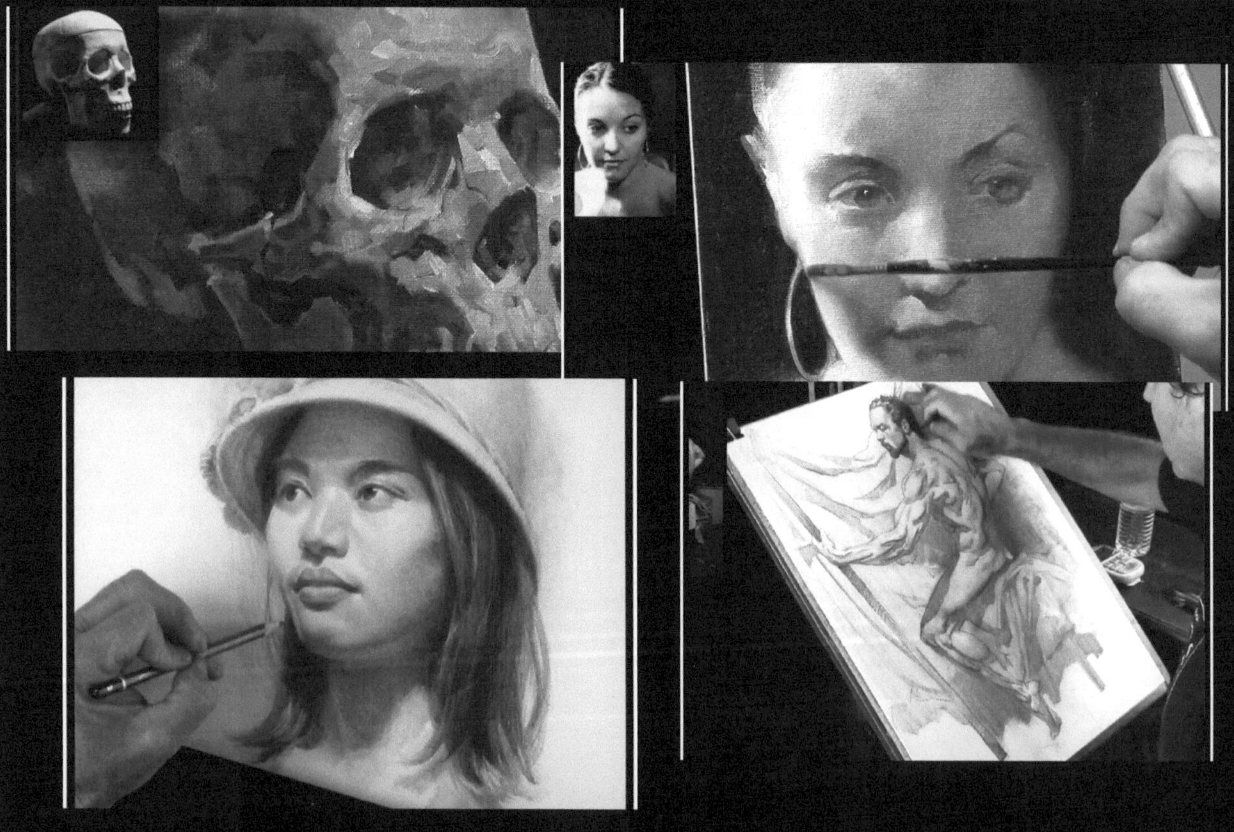

PRESERVING THE TRADITIONS OF THE MASTERS